Promoting Positive Processes after Trauma

AF755860

Promoting Positive Processes after Trauma

Elizabeth M. Altmaier
University of Iowa, Iowa City, Iowa

With contributions by
Kimberly Gleason
Des Moines, Iowa

ELSEVIER

ACADEMIC PRESS
An imprint of Elsevier

Academic Press is an imprint of Elsevier
125 London Wall, London EC2Y 5AS, United Kingdom
525 B Street, Suite 1650, San Diego, CA 92101, United States
50 Hampshire Street, 5th Floor, Cambridge, MA 02139, United States
The Boulevard, Langford Lane, Kidlington, Oxford OX5 1GB, United Kingdom

Copyright © 2019 Elsevier Inc. All rights reserved.

No part of this publication may be reproduced or transmitted in any form or by any means, electronic or mechanical, including photocopying, recording, or any information storage and retrieval system, without permission in writing from the publisher. Details on how to seek permission, further information about the Publisher's permissions policies and our arrangements with organizations such as the Copyright Clearance Center and the Copyright Licensing Agency, can be found at our website: http://www.elsevier.com/permissions.

This book and the individual contributions contained in it are protected under copyright by the Publisher (other than as may be noted herein).

Notices
Knowledge and best practice in this field are constantly changing. As new research and experience broaden our understanding, changes in research methods, professional practices, or medical treatment may become necessary.

Practitioners and researchers must always rely on their own experience and knowledge in evaluating and using any information, methods, compounds, or experiments described herein. In using such information or methods they should be mindful of their own safety and the safety of others, including parties for whom they have a professional responsibility.

To the fullest extent of the law, neither the Publisher nor the authors, contributors, or editors, assume any liability for any injury and/or damage to persons or property as a matter of products liability, negligence or otherwise, or from any use or operation of any methods, products, instructions, or ideas contained in the material herein.

British Library Cataloguing-in-Publication Data
A catalogue record for this book is available from the British Library

Library of Congress Cataloging-in-Publication Data
A catalog record for this book is available from the Library of Congress

ISBN: 978-0-12-811975-4

For Information on all Academic Press publications
visit our website at https://www.elsevier.com/books-and-journals

ELSEVIER
Book Aid International
Working together
to grow libraries in
developing countries
www.elsevier.com • www.bookaid.org

Publisher: Nikki Levy
Acquisition Editor: Joslyn Chaiprasert-Paguio
Editorial Project Manager: Megan Ashdown
Production Project Manager: Bharatwaj Varatharajan
Cover Designer: Mark Rogers

Typeset by MPS Limited, Chennai, India

Contents

Introduction **vii**

1 An introduction to trauma **1**
What is trauma? 1
How does trauma impact people? 6
What are recent contributions to trauma? 8
Summary 12
References 12
Resources for clinicians and clients 15

2 An introduction to positive psychology **17**
Positive outcomes and mechanisms of their achievement 18
Recent developments in positive psychology 21
How might trauma create growth? 24
Summary 27
References 27
Resources for clinicians and clients 30

3 Hope **31**
Defining hope 32
Hope after trauma 35
Promoting hope 37
Summary 39
References 39
Resources for clinicians and clients 41

4 Positive emotionality **43**
The role of positive emotions 44
The positive role of all emotions 47
Promoting positive emotionality 49
Summary 51
References 51
Resources for clinicians and clients 53

5 Resilience **55**
Defining resilience 56
Resilience after trauma 59

Promoting resilience 60
Summary 63
References 63
Resources for clinicians and clients 64

6 **Forgiveness** **65**
Defining forgiveness 67
Forgiveness after trauma 69
Promoting forgiveness 71
Summary 73
References 73
Resources for clinicians and clients 75

7 **Meaning in life** **77**
Defining meaning 78
Meaning after trauma 80
Promoting meaning 84
Summary 85
References 86
Resources for clinicians and clients 87

8 **Religiousness and spirituality** **89**
Defining religiousness and spirituality 90
Religiousness and spirituality after trauma 92
Promoting religiousness and spirituality 94
Summary 97
References 97
Resources for clinicians and clients 99

9 **Organization and integration of positive processes** **101**
Trajectories after trauma 102
Positive processes and life after trauma 104
Summary 107
References 108
Resources for clinicians and clients 109

Glossary of terms **111**
Index **115**

Introduction

While the term "trauma" was initially used to denote severe physical wounding of the body, it currently describes the experience by an individual of a stressor that overwhelms his or her ability to cope because of threat to life, physical health, and/or emotional health. "Trauma" refers to the event that meets certain characteristics and to the response of the persons experiencing the event. Trauma can be single events: natural disasters; terror attacks, including mass shootings; bereavement; and motor vehicle accidents. Traumas can also be repeated or even ongoing: child abuse of physical, emotional, and/or sexual natures; domestic violence; combat. As noted by Herman (1992), traumatic events "overwhelm the ordinary systems of care that give people a sense of control, connection, and meaning" (p. 33).

Personal beliefs and assumptions are the fabric of control, meaning, and connection. According to Janoff-Bulman (1989), we maintain core beliefs about the world and ourselves. First, we see the world as a benevolent place, where misfortune happens rarely. Second, we believe that life is meaningful and predictable; therefore, people "get what they deserve" (justice). Third, we see ourselves as worthwhile and decent people. Traumas create distress precisely because they cannot be accommodated within beliefs and accompanying expectations that governed life before the trauma.

The experienced consequences of trauma are symptoms, organized under diagnostic terms such as "acute stress disorder" and "post-traumatic stress disorder." These terms encompass a range of disabling phenomena, including hyperarousal and vigilance, continued and unwanted re-experiencing of the event through intrusive thoughts and images, depression and anxiety, and avoidance of situations similar to the original trauma. Traumas are usually thought about by professionals and the public within the context of dysfunction among persons who experienced them. Many traumas are increasing in frequency, and the documented likelihood of long-term deleterious impact of events such as school shootings and mass terror has brought the topic to a high level of public discourse.

In addition to this focus on the pathological, psychologists and other mental health-care professionals are emphasizing positives that can exist along with negatives in the aftermath of trauma. This concentration on positive processes was fostered by sustained attention in psychology over the last two decades to how personal strengths produce psychosocial well-being. "Positive psychology" is the umbrella term used by researchers and clinicians who study happiness and well-being among individuals and groups.

The first goal of this book is to examine strengths defined by positive psychology researchers and clinicians. In particular, these strengths are considered as they have been shown to function among trauma survivors. A second goal is to consider how clinicians can foster these strengths within their clients.

- Chapters 1 and 2 discuss foundational information on trauma and on positive psychology.
- Chapters 3 through 8 present six strengths identified by researchers and clinicians: hope, positive emotionality, resilience, forgiveness, meaning in life, and religiosity/spirituality. Each chapter defines the strength and describes relevant theory and research.
- Chapter 9 considers portfolios of positive processes, how strengths may be hierarchically organized in their relevance to trauma-dominated living, and the higher-order categories of regulatory strengths, interpersonal strengths, and meaning-making strengths.
- Supplementing and illustrating this psychological material are personal reflections from Kimberly about her own experienced trauma and her perspective about the influence of each strength in her own life. While many books contain "clinical material," this content is usually disguised summaries from clinical work or material imagined by the text's author. In contrast, Kimberly was willing to share with us her actual life experiences and insights learned during and after her trauma. Each chapter lists definitions and questions Kimberly was given. Her responses are organized to illustrate the presence and how each of the positive processes was promoted in her experience.
- At the conclusion of each chapter are additional readings and resources for the clinician and for clients.
- The text also contains a glossary of technical terms with definitions; these words are italicized in the text itself.

Elizabeth (Betsy) Altmaier earned her B.A. in Psychology from Wheaton College (IL) and her Ph.D. in Counseling Psychology from The Ohio State University. Her clinical and academic work focused on people challenged by life-threatening illness and traumatic circumstances. Her studies of persons after interpersonal trauma, patients with cancer, and patients with chronic pain led to the conclusion that finding benefit and establishing meaning results in improved physical and psychological outcomes. As a researcher, educator, and clinical supervisor, Betsy was influenced by her own life events, including childhood sexual abuse. Her recent books are *Reconstructing Meaning after Trauma* (2017a) and *Push Back the Dark: Companioning Adult Survivors of Childhood Sexual Abuse* (2017b).

Kimberly Gleason holds a B.A. in Sociology from the University of Iowa. During her time at Iowa, she was employed in the Department of Psychiatry with the Iowa Adoption Studies. Her honor's thesis investigated cohabitation, divorce, and parental divorce. Kimberly's interest in these topics was forged in personal experiences: her parents divorced when she was 4, her father had extensive cardiac problems and died when she was 19, and she experienced ongoing sexual abuse as a child. Kimberly uses her story and lessons learned from her traumas to be a positive influence on other survivors and throughout her community. This passion has led her to become a public speaker, to develop a class entitled *WalkWithMe* focused on walking alongside others in their journey of being a survivor, and to educate community centers of influence on effective response to victims of sexual violence.

The authors share the experience of trauma in our childhoods and in our adult lives. We are both deeply committed to the startling proposition that trauma creates unexpected opportunities for growth and change. Recovery after trauma requires a series of resources: connectedness, hope, identity, meaning, and empowerment. Those resources are established and sustained in the face of great loss by personal and communal strengths. Our hope is that readers of this book are empowered, equipped, and excited by the task of building those resources within the lives of persons after trauma.

References

Altmaier, E. M. (2017a). *Push back the dark: Companioning adult survivors of childhood sexual abuse*. Eugene, OR: Wipf and Stock.
Altmaier, E. M. (Ed.), (2017b). *Reconstructing meaning after trauma: Theory, research, and practice*. New York, NY: Elsevier Books.
Herman, J. (1992). *Trauma and recovery*. New York, NY: Basic Books.
Janoff-Bulman, R. (1989). Assumptive worlds and the stress of traumatic events: Application of the schema construct. *Social Cognition*, *7*, 113–136.

An introduction to trauma

1

In contemporary society, the words "trauma" and "traumatic" are ubiquitous. As an example, a search on Twitter revealed that the term "traumatic" described the following experiences: taking children to the grocery store, episodes of a television drama, a prom haircut gone wrong, and the relationship dissolution of a well-known celebrity couple. This amplified use has made it exceedingly difficult to comprehend the actual nature of trauma, an event that Herman (1992) described as follows:

> *Psychological trauma is an affliction of the powerless. At the moment of trauma, the victim is rendered helpless by overwhelming force. When the force is that of nature, we speak of disasters. When that force is that of other human beings, we speak of atrocities. Traumatic events overwhelm the ordinary systems of care that give people a sense of control, connection, and meaning. (p. 33).*

Given how many clients come for treatment with a history of trauma, having an accurate understanding of trauma is critical for responding to our clients even if they do not, themselves, cite trauma as the source of their difficulties. In society also, systems and organizations are currently adopting the perspective that working with people having past traumas must incorporate specialized elements. *Trauma-informed* is the term for this approach (see Ko et al. 2008). Systems that work for children and adults that have been re-envisioned through a trauma-informed lens are in-patient mental health settings, education, community care, critical care, substance abuse treatment, and corrections. A trauma-informed perspective is critical for clinicians as well.

This chapter reviews the history of the concept of trauma; theory and research concerning trauma, including models of how trauma creates impairment among those who experience it; and new contributions to understanding trauma. Included at the end of the chapter are recommended readings for clinicians and for their clients.

What is trauma?

The term "trauma" has been used for centuries, and is derived from a Greek word meaning wound. In its original use, "trauma" referred to physical injuries in and on the body produced by a suddenly occurring outside force; these injuries were severe, with potential to cause death or prolonged disability. Scoring systems for

Promoting Positive Processes after Trauma. DOI: https://doi.org/10.1016/B978-0-12-811975-4.00001-0
Copyright © 2019 Elsevier Inc. All rights reserved.

these physical traumas (see Lecky, Woodford, Edwards, Bouamra, & Coats, 2014) therefore focus on indicators that measure the significant damages present in the body, such as problematic changes in blood pressure and respiration rate, and severe anatomical injuries including burns, dislocations, and lacerations.

Another application of "trauma" dates to World War I, where the term was employed for significant psychological damage presumably produced by contiguous physical external forces. Jones, Fear, and Wessely (2007) describe how soldiers' prolonged exposure to horrific combat conditions resulted in psychological responses such as uncontrollable weeping, becoming mute, and memory loss. At the time, these responses were thought to be caused by the soldiers' proximity to exploding shells. The term used for these impairments was *shell shock*, reflecting the belief that the psychological deterioration came from concussive wounds.

A more recent use of "trauma" is for psychological damage from external events that do not necessarily involve physical harm. Sometimes these events are called *traumatic stressors* to reflect the understanding that these external events are not physical in nature. Examples of these stressors are losing a loved one to a violent death, experience of a mass shooting, and terror events such as 9/11 and the Boston Marathon bombings. This recent perspective is the basis for the current *Diagnostic and Statistical Manual (DSM)* (American Psychiatric Association, 2013) definition of trauma precursors of post-traumatic stress disorder (PTSD) that include:

> *witnessing, in person, the event(s) as it occurred to others; learning that the traumatic event(s) occurred to a close family member or close friend; experiencing repeated or extreme exposure to aversive details of the traumatic event(s) (e.g., first responders collecting human remains; police officers repeatedly exposed to details of child abuse).*
>
> *American Psychiatric Association, 2013.*

In current psychological research and practice, "trauma" refers to both the causative event and the range of physical and psychological responses following the event that disable the individual. Recall Herman's definition that trauma overwhelms the individual's usual control, connection, and meaning. There are many such events in our contemporary world that now are recognized as "traumatic" and meet the criterion of an overpowering experience.

Mass violence

Recognition of mass violence as a trauma experienced by more than the actual victims dates to 1966, when a sniper on the University of Texas campus killed 16 people and injured 31 others over a 90-minute period. The United States Department of Justice (United States Department of Justice, 2001) defined mass violence as follows: "An activity that involves a violent act or an act dangerous to human life… that appears to be intended to intimidate or coerce a civilian population…" (United States Department of Justice, 2001, p. 17580). Often mass violence occurs in settings that would have been considered safe by victims: a school (e.g., the

Columbine High School shooting in 1999, the Sandy Hook Elementary School shooting in 2012), a church (e.g., the Emanuel AME Church shooting in 2013), and a community location (e.g., Edmond Oklahoma post office shooting in 1986). The experience of violence in contrast to presumed safety is part of the overwhelming experience of survivors. In a parallel fashion, recent terrorist events have occurred in places associated with tourism or leisure, such as beach promenades or nightclubs.

Sexual assault

Sexual assault, or sexual violence, is a sexual act "committed or attempted by another person without freely given consent of the victim" (Centers for Disease Control, 2014b). Acts including actual sexual contact are covered in this definition. However, sexual violence incorporates other forms of assault, such as verbal coercion, and noncontact activities, such as forced viewing of pornography. Additionally, technology can be used as a means of sexual violence. At the time of the writing of this book, the Defense Department of the United States had begun a criminal investigation into a secret Facebook site used to post sexually explicit pictures of female Marines without their knowledge or consent (see Phillips, 2017 and The Guardian, 2017). The pictures were accompanied by comments regarding the women, including aggressive language and threats of sexual violence.

Peer-to-peer violence among children and adults

Peer-to-peer violence, including *bullying*, is responsible for many negative outcomes among children (e.g., physical and emotional problems, school avoidance, lowered academic achievement, behavioral problems). Peer violence includes physical attacks such as hitting or pushing, verbal attacks including name calling and teasing, relational aggression such as exclusion from a social group or perpetuation of rumors, and cyberbullying that occurs through technology. The prevalence of these activities (Turner, Finkelhor, Shattuck, Hamby, & Mitchell, 2014) is striking: about half of a sample of school-aged children have experienced at least one type or form of peer victimization in the last year.

However, peer-to-peer violence is not limited to children. In fact, work-place harassment, sometimes called *mobbing* or workplace bullying, occurs on a regular basis among adults. A definition of workplace bullying from Matthiesen and Einarsen (2007) makes it explicit that bullying is not a one-time event, and is not behavior that is trivial in nature. Rather, the imbalance of power between the persons (i.e., supervisor, worker) and their escalating conflict have negative effects on the victim in work-related indicators, such as absenteeism and sick leave, and on personal well-being indicators, such as depression and anxiety. Branch, Ramsay, and Barker (2012) outline a cyclical model of bullying that includes work environment; organizational response; and characteristics of the target, perpetrator, and bystanders which underlines the serious nature of these events for persons and for the organization.

Intimate partner violence

Intimate partner violence is the term for physical and sexual violence as well as psychological aggression and stalking perpetuated against a victim by a current or former intimate partner. The Centers for Disease Control (Centers for Disease Control & Prevention, 2014a) established not only that these traumas occur frequently, but that they also occur at an early age. In a national survey completed in 2011, approximately 54% of female victims and 47% of male victims were traumatized before age 25. Overall, in the 12 months before the survey was completed, 7% of women experienced sexual violence, 5% of women were stalked, and 5% of women experienced physical violence by a partner. The lifetime prevalence – 1 in 5 women and 1 in 7 men – and the consequences of intimate partner violence (e.g., chronic pain, binge drinking, and sexually transmitted diseases) are so severe that Mercy and Freire (2015) termed it a public health crisis.

Natural disasters and environmental disasters

Natural disasters are unavoidable environmental events that create fear of injury, loss of property, and dislocation of residence. There are many such events in the course of a single year: in 2015, for example, the National Red Cross responded to 176 disasters (Red Cross, 2015) including wildfires, floods, tornadoes, and extreme storms. In contrast, environmental disasters are caused by human and/or machine errors. Examples are oil spills and chemical plant explosions. Both natural disasters and environmental disasters take away people's access to the basic necessities of food, water, and shelter; create a need for relocation; and cause long-lasting damage to communities. In addition, consequences of disasters often occur over an extended period of time and become sequential traumas, particularly as they promote helplessness among victims.

Bereavement

The loss of a loved one to death is not an event included in the DSM definition of a trauma, but can be a traumatic stressor. Shakespeare-Finch and Armstrong (2010) demonstrated comparable levels of distress among adults who experienced sexual assault, motor vehicle accidents, and bereavement. Distress after bereavement may be influenced by the cause of death, the relationship of the deceased to the person, and the predictability of the death. For example, losing a child, or a loved one, due to suicide, or an ambiguous loss (where the lost one may be physically present but psychologically lost due to dementia or other illness) increases disabling responses to bereavement. In recognition of this potential, the DSM proposes a category for further study, Persistent Complex Bereavement Disorder. The criteria include a lengthy period (12 months for adults, 6 months for children) of intense sorrow and preoccupation, difficulty accepting the death, disruption of normal social activities, and a disturbance in identity.

Motor vehicle accidents

Motor vehicle accidents are a common occurrence in life. Unfortunately, they can create psychological disturbances, especially when the accident resulted in severe injury to driver or passenger or legal consequences such as a lawsuit. Wu and Cheung (2006) studied 600 survivors during a 6-month post-accident time period. Among those survivors, 20% reported long-term disabling effects, particularly if they experienced the accident as life-threatening. If the driver caused the death of another person, self-blame exacerbates the emotional consequences. Darin Strauss, a well-known writer, began his examination of the effects of such an accident with "Half my life ago, I killed a girl" (Strauss, 2010, p. 7).

Broader definition of trauma

We know that events discussed above occur frequently in people's lives. In fact, a national survey in the early 1990's (Kessler, Sonnega, Bromet, Hughes, & Nelson, 1995) revealed that half of the adult population experienced a major traumatic event in their lifetime, a number that increased to close to 90% in a national study conducted in 2010 (Kilpatrick et al., 2013). With near universal experience of trauma, why do some people suffer post-event impairment while others do not even while experiencing the same event?

Many scholars and practitioners have argued for a broader definition of trauma that considers it within the interaction of the event itself and the person experiencing it. One such perspective is that of Janoff-Bulman (1989), who explained trauma in terms of the shattered assumptions caused by the event. In her view, all of us maintain core beliefs about the world and our role in it. In particular, those beliefs exist in three domains. The first domain is that the world is a benevolent place; in this domain are beliefs such as "people are essentially kind" and "misfortune occurs infrequently." The second domain is that life is meaningful and not random; in this domain are beliefs such as people "get what they deserve" (justice) and "good things happen to good people and bad things happen to bad people" (controllability). The last domain is that we see ourselves as worthwhile and decent persons.

When the experienced event does not fit, and cannot be accommodated, within these beliefs, the individual feels anxious, vulnerable, and adrift. Schuler and Boals (2016) demonstrated, for example, that traumas caused college students to change their assumptions. As an example, consider a college student who is robbed while walking home alone in the evening after a class. The student experiences this assault as traumatic: not only was it frightening and threatening, but it also violated the student's beliefs that the world in general is a safe place and that bad things happen only to bad people. Thus, using earlier terms, the trauma violated core beliefs about meaningfulness (justice) and benevolence. This broader understanding of trauma as *both* an event *and* a person – where that interaction is an event that challenges the individual's ability to respond, overwhelms his or her emotions, and creates persistent distress – unifies the various types of events that have been studied as traumas and are experienced in most persons' lives.

Thus, it is understandable and even likely that individuals will not respond to situations similarly even when the same situation is experienced. Further, individuals will likely not respond similarly to situations across their lives; losing a parent to death as a child is difficult for many years while having a parent die when he or she has finished a full life, while painful in its loss, is expected. It is important for clinicians to assess both the event and how the event was experienced and understood, for in that interaction is necessary information for determining diagnosis and treatment.

How does trauma impact people?

Early research on the effects of trauma relied on studies of laboratory animals subjected to stressful and threatening stimuli. Based on laboratory studies, Cannon (1915) developed the original "fight or flight" conceptualization, in which fear caused physiological changes, such as increased blood flow, heart rate, blood pressure, and glucose stimulated by cortisol from the adrenal glands, which help the victim take flight away from a predator or fight back and attack the predator.

Recent laboratory research has established that humans have complex responses to threat. For example, Low, Weymar, and Hamm (2015) studied how autonomic responses changed due to the individual perceiving that the threat was avoidable versus unavoidable. In their study, when painful aversive stimuli (electric shock) could not be avoided, defensive freezing behaviors occurred, including a decreased heart rate. In contrast, when shock was avoidable, arousal responses occurred, including an increase in heart rate. In general, these conceptualizations center on the automatic response of the body to perceived threat: changes in skin conduction, heart rate, and startle reflexes operate to promote the individual's survival, either in immobility (freezing, fainting), in flight, or in fight.

Clinicians use the term post-traumatic stress disorder (PTSD) (APA, 2013) for traumatized persons who have symptoms, in four particular categories, which last more than one month or occur more than one month after the trauma. First are intrusive symptoms: involuntary memories, marked physiological reactions to internal or external cues that resemble or symbolize the original traumatic event, recurrent distressing dreams, and re-experiencing episodes such as flashbacks. Second, the individual persistently avoids stimuli associated with the original traumatic event, such as activities or locations. Third are increased arousal symptoms which include exaggerated startle response, self-destructive behaviors, or problems with concentration. Fourth are alterations in mood and cognitions: negative thoughts associated with the event, persistent fear, feelings of detachment from others, and negative beliefs about the self and the world.

In contrast to understanding trauma solely from the perspective of bodily and autonomic responses to threat, these symptom categories reveal the critical role of cognition and memory in impairment after trauma. Many models of trauma and of PTSD focus on how trauma memories differ from other personal memories. In a review of stories of trauma, Crespo and Fernandez-Lansac (2016) analyzed narratives from 1500 persons, primarily 20–30 years of age, who experienced a range of traumas including terrorist attacks, interpersonal abuse, and combat. Several qualities of the narratives were widely shared among participants. First, trauma narratives were disorganized and fragmented. Second, content was commonly negative in emotion and included sensory aspects of memory. Last, narratives contained more negative self-referents.

Perhaps the most pernicious effect of trauma is its ongoing damage to the whole of "living." Van der Kolk (2014) notes that an emphasis on trauma memories – thinking about how to change the past – has deprived clinicians of a necessary focus on how trauma degrades regular movement through current life. More specifically, and of central importance to the perspective in this book, is that trauma imprints people's bodies and minds in ways that damage their ongoing experience of the present.

> *"Trauma results in a fundamental reorganization of the way mind and body manage perceptions. It changes not only how we think and what we think about, but also our very capacity to think. . .The act of telling the story doesn't necessarily alter the automatic physical and hormonal responses of bodies that remain hypervigilant, prepared to be assaulted or violated at any time. For real change to take place, the body needs to learn that the danger has passed and to live in* the reality of the present.*" (italics mine; Van der Kolk, 2014, p. 21)*

Immobilization

Immobilization, or freezing, is more than a response in the midst of trauma. Immobility also occurs as the individual attempts to navigate ongoing tasks of life after the trauma. In important ways, nothing "exists" for the individual except for the trauma. Whether it is through the frequent experience of fear, or active avoidance of persons and situations, or anticipation of future negative outcomes, the life of the traumatized person is defined by the past trauma. Another way of thinking about this concept is that the individual is "stuck." He or she is no longer alive in the present because the present only exists through the filter of the trauma. The consequence of this immobilization is that the individual cannot take in and learn from new experiences, especially when that information might improve function and increase well-being.

Arousal and affect regulation

All models of post-trauma disorders emphasize the way in which the arousal system of the brain is affected. There is too much arousal, and the thinking mind shuts down. Trauma then becomes what van der Kolk called "speechless terror," an event that does not exist in language but rather in feelings. Ongoing fear, as well as increased arousal evident in hypervigilance and increased startle reactions, interfere with new learning and negatively impact quality of life. These emotions are experienced by the traumatized individual as overwhelming, beyond being coped with, and only able to be navigated through avoidance or numbing. Tedeschi and Moore (2016) portray the wide range of possible emotions that signal arousal impairment – fear, frustration, anger, disgust, apathy, guilt, fatigue, confusion, sadness, and distress.

Distortion of reality

A third significant response is that traumatized individuals do not have an accurate observing capacity. Models of how we perceive events, such as the transactional model proposed by Folkman and Lazarus (1988), apply to virtually every aspect of life: work-place difficulties, parent–child and couple interaction, and chronic illness, among many. This model considers the individual's response to an event as coming from both the event and the individual's appraisal of the event. If during initial appraisal of the event, resources (both personal and external, such as social support) are not deemed sufficient for coping with the event, then a stress response occurs. This emphasis on the role of appraisal reveals the importance of one's own map of the world. What do we perceive is available to us in the present? If our perceptions are skewed by the experience of earlier trauma, we will never see current resources as adequate for our present problems.

Identity

Too often, a trauma survivor feels defined by that event: I am an incest survivor, I am a cancer survivor. This definition can be inadvertently promoted by treatment, where the focus is the trauma and its past and present effects. The original intent of the use of "survivor" rather than "victim" in conversation and writing about abuse was to emphasize that survivors have resources, can fight back, and can take action in the face of obstacles. The term "victim" denotes passivity, something done to someone who cannot escape. However, even a survivor can be defined by the survival experience when it is the central aspect of his or her life. A traumatized person, as noted above, is stuck. The experience of being stuck also applies to how we see ourselves. Identity should be malleable, that it can and does change over time to accurately reflect new ways of being; traumatized persons have identities that are fixed, unable to accept newer or unfamiliar definitions of the self.

What are recent contributions to trauma?

Study and treatment of trauma have a relatively long history. Cannon's original conceptualizations were made in the early 1900's and the widespread recognition of psychological as well as physical damage dates to the same time period, during World War I. With each research and clinical contribution, however, it became evident that the study of trauma remained incomplete. Fortunately, significant advances in theory, research, and treatment of trauma have occurred in the last several decades. These advances were paired with an increased emphasis on trauma within relevant disciplines such as psychology; for example, the Division of Trauma Psychology was established within the American Psychological Association in 2006.

Vicarious trauma

Many professionals work with traumatized persons on a daily basis. Mental health professionals, law enforcement officers, first responders, fire fighters, and healthcare providers, among others, are on the "front lines" responding to persons in the middle of traumas including assaults, accidents, violence, and disasters. While it may have been tempting to think these responders have necessary psychological distance and are not affected by their work responsibilities, research (see Figley, 1995 for a review) reveals that working with traumatized persons causes significant distress for the responder. Several terms have been used for this distress: vicarious traumatization, secondary traumatic stress, and compassion fatigue. All of these terms encompass development of symptoms of traumatization in persons who are exposed to the experienced trauma of another, including details of the traumatic events and the victim's response.

Turgoose, Glover, Barker, and Maddux (2017) studied police officers whose responsibilities included interviewing victims of sexual exploitation, including children. Officers with more time in these responsibilities reported more distress in measures of compassion fatigue, secondary traumatic stress, and burnout than officers who had less involvement. Feedback from a training session revealed that these symptoms were not believed by officers as shared by others; rather, officers thought they were alone in having these responses to trauma. Giving these feelings a name, understanding them as normal responses shared by colleagues, and receiving organizational support for dealing with them were benefits of training.

The newest DMS-5 definition of a trauma precursor for a diagnosis of PTSD recognized this phenomenon of frequent interaction with traumatized persons, and included "experiencing repeated or extreme exposure to aversive details of the traumatic event(s)" as a potential precursor to PTSD. Further, this interaction does not necessarily need to be in person. Adams, Shakespeare-Finch, and Armstrong (2015) studied the experience of emergency medical dispatchers, persons who answer calls to emergency telephone lines. Their results demonstrated that several aspects of the position influenced vicarious trauma: dealing with the anxiety and panic of the caller, feeling connected to the caller but not knowing the eventual outcome and therefore having no resolution, and feelings of powerless and lack of control.

Betrayal trauma

The particular trauma of child sexual abuse has many consequences. One that has attracted attention from clinicians and researchers is the likelihood of an abuse survivor being revictimized physically, emotionally, or sexually during adolescence and adulthood. It would seem logical that being victimized would create a sense of caution that would mitigate future violence, but data reveal that the opposite is the case. For example, Barnes, Noll, Putnam, and Trickett (2009), through a longitudinal study, found that women abused during childhood were twice as likely to experience later sexual and physical revictimization compared to non-abused women.

Such revictimization among certain trauma survivors is hard to explain. As a possible solution, Freyd (Freyd, DePrince, & Zurbriggen, 2001; Gobin & Freyd, 2009) proposed the existence of *betrayal trauma*: an aspect of trauma that exists in addition to its severity or frequency. Traumas that involve betrayal are those perpetrated by a person who the victim trusts and on whom the victim depends. Betrayal can occur in ongoing interpersonal relationships such as family; it can also occur in organizational contexts in which mutually trusting relationships are expected, and in fact required, in order to carry out the mission of the organization. Examples are the military and church settings.

Birrell, Bernstein, and Freyd (2017) noted that cognitive processing of a traumatic event rests not only on the fear or terror it evoked, but also on the betrayal it involved. The greater the betrayal, the more the individual is likely to manifest shame and dissociation (see Platt & Freyd, 2015). Betrayal blindness is an adaptive function that allows the victim to stay in the relationship with the perpetrator, but it also functions in maladaptive ways for the victim including difficulty remembering the trauma, self-blaming for the trauma, and normalizing the trauma.

Transgenerational transmission

One group of trauma survivors who have been widely studied are Holocaust survivors. Initially, clinical observation (e.g., Nathan, Eitinger, & Winnik, 1964) of survivors of Nazi concentration camps revealed problems in functioning in everyday life after the war. These problems were emotional (e.g., depression, anxiety), interpersonal (e.g., detached social relationships, difficulties in marital and familial communication), and cognitive (e.g., difficulty in concentration) in nature. Then, these problems were also found among the children of survivors, a group termed Offspring of Holocaust Survivors (OHS). For example, Yehuda, Bell, Bierer, and Schmeidler (2008) demonstrated that OHS offspring, compared to demographically comparable Jewish controls, had more mood, anxiety, and substance use disorders.

This intergenerational trauma transmission was presumed to take place through sociobehavioral processes such as maternal emotional disturbance, child-rearing behaviors, and parent–child communication. However, in Yehuda et al. (2008), maternal PTSD was associated with increased PTSD among offspring, suggesting that pathways of influence might be biological in addition to sociobehavioral. One focus of research became genetic changes among survivors, created by environmental influences they experienced, passed on to their offspring, a process termed *epigenetic inheritance*. A recent study (Yehuda et al., 2014) was among the first to establish that Holocaust exposure created these intergenerational effects through genetic expression.

Military trauma

The role of combat in trauma has been recognized for many years. Our society is faced with mounting evidence of impairment among veterans, evident in measures such as suicide, substance abuse, and homelessness (Blow et al., 2012; Metraux, Cusack, Bryne, Hunt-Johnson, & True, 2017). It has been noted (see Litz, 2007 for review) that wars in Afghanistan and Iraq, particularly, have features that contribute to increased mental health problems. One such feature is the extent of guerilla warfare and terrorist actions from persons who appear to be civilians, thus creating a sense of ambiguity that does not abate. Another feature is improved protective body armor and medical care that has resulted in fewer deaths but greater injuries including traumatic brain injury, burns, wounds from bomb fragments, and explosive injuries.

Research reveals great variations in short- and long-term adjustment among veterans. Clinicians and researchers have attempted to identify factors, controllable and non-controllable, that affect veterans' psychological response to the trauma of combat. Some factors are experienced before deployment, notably previous adversity. Other factors are associated with combat, including degree of combat exposure. Last are factors that exist post-deployment, including lack of social support, reduced personal motivation about obtaining care, belief that emotional distress is a sign of weakness, and disability.

An additional trauma factor that has been studied is *moral injury*. During deployment, service members may be called upon to participate in, or may witness, actions that go against their own moral code. Examples of these actions are atrocities or other actions that violate usual rules of combat in that area. These actions, while not personally harmful, result in symptoms including depression, shame, and PTSD symptoms (see Drescher et al., 2011). Recent research has considered the paths of influence of the actions to the consequences. For example, Held et al. (2018) conducted interviews with veterans after deployment and analyzed their narratives for commonalities across events. Examples of these commonalities were timing (e.g., veterans knew almost immediately that the actions were morally wrong), inability to cope (e.g., using rumination, alcohol, and secrecy to cover up), and search for meaning.

Immigration

Immigration and migration are traumas occurring worldwide as the rate of immigration, legal or illegal, and of migration by refugees is at its highest since World War II. In 2015, the United Nations noted that over 60 million persons were displaced worldwide [http://www.unhcr.org/576408cd7]. Reasons for this surge are armed conflicts, particularly as those conflicts result in epidemics of hunger and disease; persecution of certain people groups; and economic instability.

The mental health of refugee and migrant people is significantly compromised by pre-migration events, the difficulties of transit, and post-migration and settlement uncertainties. Traumas are widespread during these stages. For example, Shannon, Vinson, Wieling, Cook, and Letts (2015) reported on war trauma and mental health among refugees from Burma who completed a public health screening in the United States. Before their migration, 30% of respondents experienced torture, and virtually all the respondents reported war traumas of forced labor, destruction of homes, bombing, and injury. In-transit traumas (Hall & Olff, 2016) were also common: being attacked and injured, witnessing violence, and fearing death. Time in refugee camps or other temporary locations created instability and uncertain futures. Even on resettlement, adapting to a new country, language, customs and culture are challenging.

Given these extreme difficulties, it is not surprising that refugees exhibit high levels of depression, PTSD, and anxiety. A large-scale analysis of studies (Steel et al., 2009) revealed the average prevalence of these disorders was approximately 30%. A further concern is that traumas experienced before, during, and after migration pose threats to longer-term mental health, and increase in the likelihood of delayed physical health concerns.

Summary

Traumatic events create a range of after-effects. Some of these after-effects are challenging, but transient. Bonanno (2004) argued that human capacity to respond resiliently after trauma may be underappreciated. Data that he summarizes demonstrated that trajectories after trauma suggest both resilience and recovery. However, the increasing frequency of societal events that are traumatic in their impact, and the likelihood of deleterious long-term impacts of those events, underline the importance of keeping a trauma-informed focus in clinical work specifically and human services more generally.

This chapter describes the development of the conceptualization of trauma, notes its pervasive presence in everyday life, and summarizes negative consequences of trauma. Addressing questions about trauma has encouraged contemporary researchers and clinicians to develop new models of trauma, which in turn suggest additional factors to assess in the traumatic background and about the individual response. This book focuses in particular on difficulties experienced by the traumatized person in his or her effective living in the present moment, and on ways in which positive psychology has identified resources to resolve those difficulties.

References

Adams, K., Shakespeare-Finch, J., & Armstrong, D. (2015). An interpretative phenomenological analysis of stress and well-being in emergency medical dispatchers. *Journal of Loss and Trauma*, *20*, 430–448.

Akhila. (2012, March 13). Why words matter: Victim v. Survivor. [Web log comment]. Available from <https://survivornotvictim.com/blog/2017/6/30/why-your-choice-of-words-do-matter>.

American Psychiatric Association. (2013). *Diagnostic and statistical manual of mental disorders* (5th edition). Washington, DC: American Psychiatric Association Publishing.

Barnes, J. E., Noll, J. G., Putnam, F. W., & Trickett, P. K. (2009). Sexual and physical revictimization among victims of severe childhood sexual abuse. *Child Abuse & Neglect*, *33*, 412–420.

Birrell, P. J., Bernstein, R. E., & Freyd, J. J. (2017). With the fierce and loving embrace of another soul: Finding connection and meaning after the profound disconnection of betrayal trauma. In E. M. Altmaier (Ed.), *Reconstructing meaning after trauma* (pp. 29–43). New York, NY: Elsevier.

Blow, F. C., Bohnert, A. S. B., Ilgen, M. A., Ignacio, R., McCarthy, J. F., Valenstein, M. M., & Knox, K. L. (2012). Suicide mortality among patients treated by the Veterans Health Administration from 2000 to 2007. *American Journal of Public Health, 102*, S98–S104.

Bonanno, G. (2004). Loss, trauma, and human resilience: Have we underestimated the human capacity to thrive after extremely aversive events? *American Psychologist, 59*, 20–28.

Branch, S., Ramsay, S., & Barker, M. (2012). Workplace bullying, mobbing and general harassment: A review. *International Journal of Management Reviews, 15*, 280–299.

Cannon, W. B. (1915). *Bodily changes in pain, hunger, fear and rage: An account of recent researches into the function of emotional excitement*. New York, NY: Appleton and Co.

Centers for Disease Control and Prevention. (2014a). *Prevalence and characteristics of sexual violence, stalking, and intimate partner violence victimization – National Intimate Partner and Sexual Violence Survey, United States, 2011*. Available from <https://www.cdc.gov/mmwr/preview/mmwrhtml/ss6308a1.htm?s_cid = ss6308a1_e>.

Centers for Disease Control and Prevention. (2014b). Sexual violence surveillance: Uniform definitions and recommended data elements. Available from https://www.cdc.gov/violenceprevention/pdf/sv_surveillance_definitionsl-2009-a.pdf.

Crespo, M., & Fernandez-Lansac, V. (2016). Memory and narrative of traumatic events: A literature review. *Psychological Trauma: Theory, Research, Practice, and Policy, 8*, 149–156.

Drescher, K. D., Foy, D. W., Kelly, C., Leshner, A., Schutz, K., & litz, B. (2011). An exploration of the viability and usefulness of the construct of moral injury in war veterans. *Traumatology, 17*, 8–13.

Figley, C. R. (Ed.), (1995). *Compassion fatigue: Coping with secondary traumatic stress disorder in those who treat the traumatized*. Philadelphia, PA: Brunner/Mazel.

Folkman, S., & Lazarus, R. S. (1988). Coping as a mediator of emotion. *Journal of Personality and Social Psychology, 54*, 466–475.

Freyd, J., DePrince, A. P., & Zurbriggen, E. L. (2001). Self-reported memory for abuse depends on victim-perpetrator relationship. *Journal of Trauma & Dissociation, 2*, 5–16.

Gobin, R. L., & Freyd, J. J. (2009). Betrayal and revictimization: Preliminary findings. *Psychological Trauma: Theory, Research, Practice, and Policy, 1*, 242–257.

Hall, B. J., & Olff, M. (2016). Global mental health: trauma and adversity among populations in transition. *European Journal of Psychotraumatology, 7*, 31140.

Held, P., Klassen, B. J., Hall, J. M., Triese, T. R., Bertsch-Gout, M. M., Zalta, A. K., & Pollack, M. H. (2018). "I knew it was wrong the moment I got the order": A narrative thematic analysis of moral injury in combat veterans. *Psychological Trauma: Theory, Research, Practice, and Policy*.

Herman, J. (1992). *Trauma and recovery*. New York, NY: Basic Books.

Janoff-Bulman, R. (1989). Assumptive worlds and the stress of traumatic events: Applications of the schema concept. *Social Cognition, 7*, 113–136.

Jones, E., Fear, N. T., & Wessely, S. (2007). Shell shock and mild traumatic brain injury: A historical review. *American Journal of Psychiatry, 164*, 1641–1645.

Kessler, R. C., Sonnega, A., Bromet, E., Hughes, M., & Nelson, C. B. (1995). Posttraumatic stress disorder in the National Comorbidity Survey. *Archives of General Psychiatry, 52*, 1048–1060.

Kilpatrick, D. G., Resnick, H. S., Milanak, M. E., Miller, M. W., Keyes, K. M., & Friedman, J. J. (2013). National estimates of exposure to traumatic events and PTSD prevalence using DSM-IV and DSM-5 criteria. *Journal of Traumatic Stress*, *26*, 537–547.

Ko, S. J., Ford, J. D., Kassam-Adams, N., Berkowitz, S. J., Wilson, C., Wong, M., ... Layne, C. M. (2008). Creating trauma-informed systems: Child welfare, education, first responders, health care, juvenile justice. *Professional Psychology: Research and Practice*, *39*, 396–404.

Lecky, F., Woodford, M., Edwards, A., Bouamra, O., & Coats, T. (2014). Trauma scoring systems and databases. *British Journal of Anaesthesia*, *113*, 286–294.

Litz, B. T. (2007). Research on the impact of military trauma: Current status and future directions. *Military Psychology*, *19*, 217–238.

Low, A., Weymar, M., & Hamm, A. O. (2015). When threat is near, get out of here: Dynamics of defensive behavior during freezing and active avoidance. *Psychological Science*, *26*, 1706–1716.

Matthiesen, S., & Einarsen, S. (2007). Perpetrators and targets of bullying at work: Role stress and individual differences. *Violence and Victims*, *22*, 735–753.

Mercy, J. A., & Freire, K. E. (2015). DELTA PREP: Building capacity to meet the public health urgency of intimate partner violence. *Health Education & Behavior*, *42*, 433–435.

Metraux, S., Cusack, M., Bryne, T. H., Hunt-Johnson, N., & True, G. (2017). Pathways into homelessness among post-9/11 era veterans. *Psychological Sciences*, *14*, 229–237.

Nathan, T. S., Eitinger, L., & Winnik, H. Z. (1964). A psychiatric study of survivors of the Nazi Holocaust: A study in hospitalized patients. *Israel Annals of Psychiatry & Related Disciplines*, *2*, 47–76.

Phillips, D. (2017, March 6). Inquiry opens into how 30,000 Marines shared illicit images of female peers. *The New York Times*. Available from <https://www.nytimes.com/2017/03/06/us/inquiry-opens-into-how-30000-marines-shared-illicit-images-of-female-peers.html>.

Platt, M. G., & Freyd, J. J. (2015). Betray my trust, shame on me: Shame, dissociation, fear, and betrayal trauma. *Psychological Trauma: Theory, Research, Practice, and Policy*, *7*, 398–404.

Red Cross. (2015). http://www.redcross.org/news/press-release/Red-Cross-Responded-to-176-Large-US-Disasters-in-2015.

Schuler, E. R., & Boals, A. (2016). Shattering world assumptions: A prospective view of the impact of adverse events on world assumptions. *Psychological Trauma: Theory, Research, Practice, and Policy*, *8*, 259–266.

Shakespeare-Finch, J., & Armstrong, D. (2010). Trauma type and posttrauma outcomes: Differences between survivors of motor vehicle accidents, sexual assault, and bereavement. *Journal of Loss and Trauma*, *15*, 69–82.

Shannon, P. J., Vinson, G. A., Wieling, E., Cook, R., & Letts, J. (2015). Torture, war trauma, and mental health symptoms of newly arrived Karen refugees. *Journal of Loss and Trauma*, *20*, 577–590.

Steel, Z., Chey, T., Silove, D., Marnane, C., Bryant, R. A., & van Ommeren, M. (2009). Association of torture and other potentially traumatic events with mental health outcomes among populations exposed to mass conflict and displacement: A systematic review and meta-analysis. *Journal of the American Medical Association*, *302*, 537–549.

Strauss, D. (2010). *Half a life*. San Francisco, CA: McSweeneys.

Tedeschi, R. G., & Moore, B. A. (2016). *The posttraumatic growth workbook*. Oakland, CA: New Harbinger Publications.

The Guardian, March 6, 2017. Available from <https://www.theguardian.com/us-news/2017/mar/06/us-military-investigates-secret-distasteful-facebook-page-of-naked-female-marines>.

Turgoose, D., Glover, N., Barker, C., & Maddux, L. (2017). Empathy, compassion fatigue, and burnout among police officers working with rape victims. *Traumatology, 23*, 205–213.

Turner, H. A., Finkelhor, D., Shattuck, A., Hamby, S., & Mitchell, K. (2014). Beyond bullying: Aggravating elements of peer victimization episodes. *School Psychology Quarterly, 30*, 366–384.

United States Department of Justice. (2001). Antiterrorism and emergency fund guidelines for terrorism and mass violence crimes. *Federal Register, 66*(63), 17577–17583.

Van der Kolk, B. (2014). *The body keeps the score*. New York, NY: Penguin Group.

Wu, K. K., & Cheung, M. W. L. (2006). Posttraumatic stress after a motor vehicle accident: A six-month follow-up study utilizing latent growth modeling. *Journal of Traumatic Stress, 19*, 923–936. Available from https://doi.org/10.1002/jts.20178.

Yehuda, R., Bell, A., Bierer, L. M., & Schmeidler, J. (2008). Maternal, not paternal, PTSD is related to increased risk for PTSD in offspring of Holocaust survivors. *Journal of Psychiatric Research, 42*, 1104–1111.

Yehuda, R., Daskalakis, N. P., Lehrner, A., Desarnoud, F., Bader, H. N., Makotkine, I., ... Meaney, M. J. (2014). Influences of maternal and paternal PTSD on epigenetic regulation of the glucocorticoid receptor gene in Holocaust survivor offspring. *The American Journal of Psychiatry, 171*, 872–880.

Resources for clinicians and clients

Brewin, C. R., Andrews, B., & Valentine, J. D. (2000). Meta-analysis of risk factors for posttraumatic stress disorder in trauma-exposed adults. *Journal of Consulting and Clinical Psychology, 68*, 748–766.

Curran, L. A. (2010). *Trauma competency: A clinician's guide*. Eau Claire, WI: PESI LLC.

Follette, V. M., & Pistorello, J. (2007). *Finding life beyond trauma: Using acceptance and commitment therapy to heal from posttraumatic stress and trauma-related problems*. Oakland, CA: New Harbinger Publications.

Lord, J. H., Hook, M., Alkhateeb, S., & English, S. J. (2008). *Spiritually sensitive caregiving: A multi-faith handbook*. Burnsville, NC: Compassion Press.

Segerstrom, S. C., & Miller, G. E. (2004). Psychological stress and the human immune system: A meta-analytic study of 30 years of inquiry. *Psychological Bulletin, 130*, 601–630.

Silverman, W. K., Ortiz, C. D., Viswesvaran, C., Burns, B., Kolko, D. J., Putnam, F. W., & Amaya-Jackson, L. (2008). Evidence-based psychosocial treatments for children and adolescents exposed to traumatic events. *Journal of Clinical and Adolescent Psychology, 37*, 156–183.

Van der Kolk, B. A., Roth, S., Pelcovitz, D., Sunday, S., Spinazzola, J., & Courtois, C. A. (2005). Disorders of extreme stress: The empirical foundation of a complex adaptation to trauma. *Journal of Traumatic Stress, 18*, 389–399.

An introduction to positive psychology

2

During the first half of the 20th century, psychologists focused their attention on assisting a wide variety of people, including persons who were not impaired as well as persons with life difficulties. For example, early psychologists (e.g., Parsons, 1909) established agencies to assist young adults in making a vocational choice while others (e.g., Witmer, 1913) helped children with academic problems. Across psychology, there was an emphasis on *hygiology* – those aspects of personality that are effective even in the presence of life's adversities – and psychology was devoted to making the lives of all people more successful.

That view of the proper scope of psychology's work changed in the second half of the 20th century when psychology became more concerned with *pathology*, aspects of personality that are abnormal and maladaptive. Further, these pathologies were believed to be different – not just in degree, but in kind – from problems experienced by nonclinical persons. This belief was the beginning of a differentiation between persons who were perceived as "normal" and those perceived as "abnormal." A *disease model* was used to understand abnormality, where problems were presumed to be located inside a person. Treatment, therefore, consisted of identifying the pathology (the disease) and prescribing a method to cure the pathology and resolve the disease. This model was borrowed from the field of medicine.

Adoption of the disease model resulted in sustained attention to causes of psychopathology, its trajectories of development, and factors that influenced its development and maintenance. Any textbook on abnormal psychology (see Beidel, Bulik, & Stanley, 2014) describes disorders by which people manifest significant pathologies. There are emotional disorders, such as anxiety and depression. There are disorders of experience, such as schizophrenia and neurocognitive disorders. Abuse of substances, including drugs and alcohol, and other addictions are increasingly prevalent concerns of our society. And the rapidly progressing number of elderly in our society has fostered a concentration on disorders of later life, including Alzheimer's disease and dementia.

In modern life, over the past few decades, the incidence of certain types of disorders appears to be rapidly increasing. Case and Deaton (2017) discussed dramatic changes in causes of adult mortality: deaths from chronic health conditions, such as cardiovascular disease, have leveled but deaths due to three particular causes – overdoses from alcohol, prescription drugs, and illegal drugs; suicide; and alcohol-related liver disease – have increased. Most importantly, these changes are not observed in countries that are economically comparable to the United States, and

Promoting Positive Processes after Trauma. DOI: https://doi.org/10.1016/B978-0-12-811975-4.00002-2
Copyright © 2019 Elsevier Inc. All rights reserved.

thus seem to underline a rise in this country of what are called "diseases of despair." It appears that in spite of psychology's attention to the pathological, success in helping people live more effective lives has not been achieved.

The emphasis of this text is *positive psychology*, a field that formally began in the late 1990's and was defined by the publication in 2000 of an "introduction" to positive psychology (Seligman & Csikszentmihalyi, 2000). Positive psychology is "not just the study of disease, weakness, and damage; it is also the study of strength and virtue" (p. 4) (Seligman, 2002). Within positive psychology are examinations of positive experiences, positive individual characteristics, and positive institutions that foster these characteristics and experiences. As noted by Duckworth, Steen, and Seligman (2005), it might seem peripheral to the very real problems of society to attend to personal and cultural strengths. However, researchers and clinicians in the positive psychology tradition note that individuals are more than their burdens: everyone wants to experience more joy, satisfaction, and accomplishment in their lives; to build their personal strengths; and to live and work in systems that promote happiness and engagement.

Traumatic events are many, and their influence is pervasive. However, it is the thesis of this text that concepts developed, articulated, and promulgated under the label of positive psychology can serve as positive processes for the difficulties of living in *the reality of the present* (Van der Kolk, 2014). And when these processes related to development, emotion, cognition, and social relationships are promoted in the lives of persons who are despairing, there will be growth and increased well-being.

Positive outcomes and mechanisms of their achievement

What is "the good life?" One view of the good life is hedonic, that is, what makes life worth living is what makes life pleasant and happy. Research within the hedonic view typically used *subjective well-being* as the measure of happiness. Diener (Diener, 1984; Diener and Lucas (1999) identified three components of subjective well-being: high levels of positive emotions, low levels of negative emotions, and high levels of life satisfaction. Subjective well-being, as indicated by its title, is measured subjectively: what one person finds pleasurable, another may not. Some individuals, too, are more generally oriented to seeking that which makes them happy (Peterson, Park, & Seligman, 2005) over that which leads to meaning or that which facilitates engagement.

In contrast to the hedonic view are eudaimonic models, where happiness occurs when one has meaning or purpose in life. Ryff (1989, Ryff & Keyes, 1995), for example, outlined a model that focuses on *flourishing*, fully realizing one's own potential. In Ryff's model, there are six aspects of happiness or well-being:

Self-acceptance: A high level of self-acceptance is signified by having a positive attitude toward oneself, including accepting qualities both "good" and "bad" as defined by the individual. In contrast, a low level of self-acceptance occurs as the individual is displeased with the self, yearns to be different, and feels great disappointment about the past.

Personal growth: Strong personal growth is associated with openness to new experiences, being challenged about the world, and seeing desired changes in oneself over time. A lack of personal growth is giving up on changes or improvements and thereby experiencing a degree of "being trapped" in life.

Purpose in life: Goals and objectives are signs of a high level of purpose in life. Believing that life is meaningful and seeing direction for oneself leads to those goals and objectives. In contrast, a low level of purpose in life is tied to having few goals, and believing that life has no direction.

Positive relations with others: Relationships are key to well-being. Strong relationships are satisfying, mutual, and trusting, and these relationships lead to intimacy. Weak interpersonal relationships occur as the individual is isolated and suspicious, and has few ties to others.

Environmental mastery: High levels of mastery are associated with competence, forming personally suitable communities and systems, and managing complex environments. Low mastery occurs as the individual has difficulty in both simple and complex decisions and actions, feels out of control and ineffective, and experiences everyday life solely as a series of demands.

Autonomy: Individuals with high levels of autonomy are self-regulating, making changes as they judge are best based on their own beliefs and values; they evaluate themselves by personal standards rather than by pressures from social contexts. Low levels of autonomy are associated with conformity to outside pressure, over-concern with others' expectations, and over-reliance on others to make one's own decisions.

Seligman (2017) recently outlined a comprehensive model of happiness that combined pleasure (hedonism) with engagement (eudaimonia). In his model (*PERMA*), positive emotions are one contributor to happiness. A second is engagement, the ability and opportunity to be absorbed into the present moment. Interpersonal relationships are the third contributor, and meaning is the fourth. Last, accomplishments that are the result of setting and reaching realistic and meaningful goals are an element of happiness. The acronym PERMA stands for positive emotion, engagement, relationships, meaning, and accomplishment and suggests that blending hedonic and eudaimonic goals results in the most happiness.

As philosophers and researchers dispute the correctness of one model over the other, people also vary in their own definitions of the good life and in their focus on hedonic or eudaimonic goals. Huta and Ryan (2010) considered five specific outcomes from activities that were motivated by hedonic and eudaimonic goals: positive and negative affect, carefreeness, meaning, "elevated experience," and vitality. In a series of studies, participants in activities motivated by hedonic goals (happiness goals) experienced an increase in positive affect in the short term, but not at a three month follow-up. In contrast, participants in activities motivated by eudaimonic goals (flourishing goals) did not experience positive affect in the short term, but reported doing so at the follow-up. Meaning and elevated experience were outcomes related to activities motivated by eudaimonia, while carefreeness was an outcome associated with activities motivated by hedonia. Finally, life satisfaction was an outcome of both types of motivations.

Positive psychology does not ignore the negative in life. Traumas occur; people's well-being is tested or even shattered; and building positive emotions, experiences, and institutions is an ongoing challenge. In fact, McMahan et al. (2016) investigated whether the belief that happiness can only occur in the absence of negative experiences was itself a possible influence on consequences of life stress. In their research, three studies were conducted with adults in two countries. Using both prospective and retrospective designs, life stress was associated with more depressive symptoms among people who endorsed *negative hedonic beliefs* (beliefs that happiness occurs only in the complete absence of pain) than with people who believed that happiness can exist in the presence of pain.

Mechanisms by which individuals bring about good outcomes under all life circumstances are termed *strengths* in positive psychology. As described by Peterson and Park (2009) and Peterson and Seligman (2004), strengths are more than personality traits. Rather, they are components of being human that have been valued across many cultures and time periods. A set of associated strengths defines a *virtue*. Building strengths increases the possession of the virtues. While everyone has all of these strengths to a greater or lesser degree, each person has a pattern of strengths that is his or hers alone.

Wisdom: Within this virtue are strengths that encompass acquisition and use of knowledge. These strengths are creativity, curiosity, open-mindedness, love of learning, and perspective. As an example, the specific strength of curiosity is the practice of approaching situations from personal interest, having a positive motivation toward atypical experiences and persons.

Courage: The strengths of the virtue of courage increase the likelihood of an individual persisting in the face of obstacles: bravery, persistence, integrity, and vitality. The strength of persistence, for example, is that which motivates an individual to finish tasks once started in spite of barriers encountered along the way.

Humanity: The virtue of humanity encompasses strengths that benefit others with whom we are in relationships. Specific strengths are love, kindness, and social intelligence. Social intelligence, for example, is when individuals accurately understand the feelings and motivations of others.

Justice: An effective community is built by strengths within the virtue of justice: teamwork, fairness, and leadership. Positive psychology is concerned with positive institutions as well as positive individuals, and these strengths create and maintain these positive institutions.

Temperance: Strengths that mitigate against excess in life are within the category of temperance. These are forgiveness, humility, prudence, and self-regulation. For example, humility is the strength of forgoing promotion of one's own accomplishments.

Transcendence: Strengths within the virtue of transcendence promote connections to the meaningful and to the spiritual in the larger universe. Gratitude, hope, humor, appreciation of beauty, and spirituality are the transcendent strengths. Hope, for example, is expecting the best in the present and future, and implementing activities necessary for the best to occur.

Strengths are more tangible expressions than virtues. They are concrete ways to talk about the manifestation of the virtue in one's own or another's life. Strengths also are multifaceted, encompassing thoughts, feelings, and actions. While all strengths are valuable, are any strengths more important than others? Boehm and Lyubomirsky (2009) noted that happiness is a combination of one's set point, life circumstances, and intentional activity. The most effective intentional activities, likeliest to increase happiness, focus on expressing and increasing the strengths of gratitude, kindness, vitality, and perspective.

As Lopez and Snyder (2009) wrote,

> *"Positive psychology is the 'scientific study' of what makes life most worth living. It is a call for psychological science and practice to be as concerned with strength as with weakness; as interested in building the best things in life as in repairing the worst; and as concerned with making the lives of normal people fulfilling as with healing pathology" (p. xxiii).*

Recent developments in positive psychology

There are several new developments in research and application that are relevant to considering the resources identified by positive psychology.

Self-compassion as a mechanism of influence

Many constructs considered in research and scholarship in a positive psychology framework are influential predictors of well-being. This text introduces the reader to six of them, but that is only a representative selection. A challenge for clinicians is to identify which of the many constructs might be most helpful for any one client. The resources section at the end of this chapter contains a survey of virtues that clients find useful. An alternative approach to promoting particular strengths is to promote a construct that provides a route for greater influence by all strengths: *self-compassion*. As defined by Neff (2003), self-compassion is being open to one's own suffering, not avoiding it or disconnecting from it. Self-compassion also speaks to a nonjudgmental way in which one's thoughts about the self are held.

Neff (2003) identified three aspects of self-compassion that buffer the individual against negative aspects of trauma, and facilitate the positive influence of other strengths. One is self-kindness: giving oneself kindness and understanding rather than hard criticism. A second is common humanity: seeing oneself and one's experiences as part of humanity rather than seeing them as isolating. A third is mindfulness: rather than overidentifying with and becoming fixated on one's thoughts and feelings, self-compassionate individuals hold distressing thoughts and feelings in a balanced awareness that neither runs toward them or away from them.

Recent research suggests self-compassion directly influences well-being and also buffers against distress. For example, Trompetter, Kleine, and de Bohlmeijer (2017) surveyed over 300 adults and found that self-compassion functioned as a mediator between negative affect and well-being, thus serving as a resilience resource. A more direct test of the role of self-compassion and trauma was conducted by Seligowski, Miron, and Orcutt (2015). In their study of trauma-exposed college students, both a nonjudgmental acceptance of oneself and a willingness to be aware of thoughts and emotions resulted in better psychological health. Thus, encouraging self-compassion among trauma survivors may assist greater influence by other strengths as well.

Crossing cultures in positive psychology

As noted by Linley and Leontiev (2009), research in positive psychology has turned to considering whether happiness, flourishing, and the "good life" are appropriate concepts cross-culturally. For example, is the "good life" the same in every country or culture? Do all cultures desire happiness as a primary goal? Wierzbicka (2009) observed from a linguistic perspective that "good life" cannot be exactly translated from English into other languages, let alone stand for parallel meanings. It is important to consider cultural relevance in today's emphasis on global citizenship, and in psychology's increased attention to multiple countries and cultures. Current work in positive psychology considers two issues in this area.

The first issue is whether positive psychology's approach to defining strengths should focus on strengths presumed to be *universal* (similar across all cultures) or known to be *culturally embedded* (can only be viewed from a cultural context and will differ greatly across cultures). A universal view would propose, for example, that all persons desire happiness as a primary goal (see Myers & Diener, 1995). Alternately, the embedded view would argue that happiness exists in various forms due to cultural expectations, and the salience of happiness itself changes due to those culturally formed expectations in a person's life. For example, in an individualistic culture that prizes autonomy, happiness might occur through achieving personal goals. In contrast, in a collectivistic culture, happiness might be anticipated as a result of conformity to familial goals, and would be a secondary or even irrelevant outcome of that conformity.

A second issue is whether advances in positive psychology should rely on particular research methodologies, those that are primarily positivistic and appear not to take into account the researcher's own possibly biased perspective. Christopher and Hickinbottom (2008) argued that significant problems occur when positive psychology is conflated with particular empirical research methodologies. In that conflation, psychology ignores how culture influences both science and the scientist. They noted that "positive psychology is doomed to being narrow and ethnocentric as long as its researchers remain unaware of the cultural assumptions underlying their work" (p. 565).

Religion and positive psychology

Many of the concepts articulated by positive psychology researchers and clinicians – such as forgiveness, humility, self-control – may appear to be grounded in moral philosophy or in religion. However, consideration of these concepts by positive psychologists has been largely devoid of infusion from scholarship from the psychology of religion and therefore has not benefited from cross-disciplinary scholarship.

In a special issue of the *Psychology of Religion and Spirituality* (Schnitker & Emmons, 2017), various authors explored conceptual and empirical overlap between the psychology of religion and positive psychology, focusing on constructs common to both; examples are humility, positive emotions such as love, and patience. In that issue, authors noted that while the two traditions have differing definitions and research methods, there are contributions each can make to the other. Charry and Kosits (2017) suggested that for theology, positive psychology creates a necessary and morally acceptable role for happiness and pleasure, enhances attention on individual differences, and embraces positive emotions. In return, theology can give positive psychology a focus on weakness as a mark of maturity, the advantages of self-examination, and the positives of negative emotions.

Interestingly in religious studies, there has also been some refocus away from sin and human helplessness. Charry (2011), for example, outlines how a pathology-driven narrative in theology might be augmented with a strengths-based narrative. In the latter, God provides resources for self-confidence and empowerment. Additionally, encouragement can be a defined purpose of religious rituals (e.g., baptism, receiving the Eucharist) rather than a singular focus on conviction of sin and failing.

Positive organizational behavior

As noted above, positive psychology includes organizations and communities within its focus. Given the amount of time we spend in work environments, "positive organizations" are an important consideration in positive psychology. A primary emphasis is work-related flourishing or thriving – how exceptional performance achieved by individuals is defined beyond traditional outcomes such as total sales, customer satisfaction, or employee persistence. Rather, positive organizational scholarship describes how human potential is elevated through work systems. As an example, the Center for Positive Organizations at the University of Michigan <positiveorgs.bus.umich.edu> states as its purpose "to inspire and enable leaders to build high-performing organizations that bring out the best in people."

Many aspects of contemporary work environments pose challenges to this goal of bringing out the best in people. For example, working remotely is a trend that accelerated over time with improvements in technology. A recent Gallup News poll (Gallup News, 2017) found that 31% of workers spend more than 80% of their work time working remotely, and an additional 11% spend 60–80% remotely. These isolating conditions offer challenges to engagement, development, and satisfaction.

A positive approach to the challenges of isolation and disengagement is the choice of *coworking* – shared space where several individuals do their own work, for different companies with different projects, but share workspace and resources.

What makes coworking different from similar environments in public spaces (e.g., coffee shops) is the intentional goal of creating a community. Garrett, Spreitzer, and Bacevice (2017) analyzed how workers fostered this community and three actions motivated by this goal. The first was endorsing a shared vision, actions that begin when people enter the coworking environment and continue through mutual bonds. The second was encountered community, an explicit recognition that people would express this shared vision differently; some would be more active, others less involved. The third was engagement in the community, varying from shared routines such as coffee and lunch breaks to social events to community service.

Positive psychology interventions

The focus of this book is not on specific interventions to increase strengths associated with positive psychology. There are such interventions, and a few are listed in the resources section. But a new direction in this field is important to consider as an adjunct to an individualistic context, and that is dyadic intervention. In dyadic intervention, the focus is on increasing strengths in the relationship between persons in order to promote adaptation to life change, rather than a focus on increasing strengths in separate people.

As an example, Krakauer (2018) administered gratitude interventions to high-conflict couples selected from a clinic setting. Over eight weeks, couples reported improved satisfaction and gratitude in their relationship. Terrill et al. (2018) tested a positive psychology intervention for couples where one partner had recently had a stroke and was receiving caregiving from the other partner. In the intervention, the couples completed activities together each week which included expressing gratitude, focusing on spirituality, practicing kindness, and working toward a goal. In addition to their results demonstrating the feasibility of working with the couple, data revealed that depression decreased over time, while quality of life in many domains increased.

How might trauma create growth?

It is evident that traumas of many types result in significant impairment across life domains. However, researchers have demonstrated that individuals vary in reactions after trauma. Bonanno (2004), for example, outlined four possible trajectories. Two of these describe development of significant distress and dysfunction after trauma: the *chronic impairment* trajectory, and the *delayed distress* trajectory in which impairments begin at a time point after the event. A third trajectory is *recovery*, where the individual experiences moderate or even severe symptoms of distress after the trauma, but those symptoms lessen over time. The fourth trajectory is *resilience*, in which the individual shows little change from the level of function displayed before the event.

Researchers (see Linley & Joseph, 2005, and Joseph & Linley, 2008) focused on a wide variety of traumas, including natural disasters and sexual assault, have documented that not all individuals experiencing trauma suffer ongoing impairment; rather, there can be adaptation to trauma experienced as positive change. In contrast to the view that considers the only positive outcome of trauma as the return to normal, or pre-trauma function, is the view that enduring positive psychological change can follow from the individual's struggles in the aftermath of traumatic or challenging events. Tedeschi and Calhoun (1995, 1996, and 2004) posited *post-traumatic growth* as positive changes in the individual after trauma. These changes or transformations occur in specific life domains: an altered sense of self, changed interpersonal relationships, and a different philosophy of life.

Sense of self: Trauma causes an increased sense of vulnerability and fear. However, after trauma, individuals have also rated themselves as stronger, seeing their survival as evidence of their capacity and resilience. They may view themselves as "better people" and endorse having confidence in themselves when they experience future traumas.

Interpersonal relationships: Traumatized persons report distance and isolation from others. But trauma can also result in improved relationships with others, especially as the trauma victim gains increased sensitivity and empathy for others in similar situations. Sometimes trauma prompts a reconsideration of difficult relationships, and a move toward reconciliation in them.

Philosophy of life: Many trauma survivors report dramatically altered priorities in life. Life may be no longer taken for granted, "small things" may be more fully appreciated, and spirituality may take a larger place in life. Meaning-making, making sense of the trauma, is also infused into life directions. Sometimes, completely new directions, in careers or in life, are also initiated after trauma.

Benefit finding is a byproduct of the trauma experience. For example, in a study (Tallman, Altmaier, & Garcia, 2007) of patients after the diagnosis and treatment of cancer, individual interviews with patients 1 and 3 years after treatment revealed a range of benefits reported by the patients. The most common benefit, at both time points, was renewed appreciation for life itself. Learning something new about oneself was also a common benefit, as was experiencing positive changes in relationships with family and/or friends. Less common were creating new directions in life, such as a change in careers.

Early perspectives on post-traumatic growth considered it an outcome of cognitive processing. As noted by Tallman (2011), outcome models presume that the traumatic event is severe enough to pose a significant challenge to one's world view, the individual has the capacity to cognitively process that challenge, and the individual has traits such as openness that allow him or her to assimilate the trauma. In support of that view, Li et al. (2018) studied post-traumatic growth predicted by rumination (both deliberate and intrusive) among hemodialysis patients. Deliberate rumination was positively correlated with later growth, while intrusive rumination was negatively correlated.

Process models, on the other hand, consider post-traumatic growth as the process by which individuals construct personal benefit and meaning from the trauma. Park and Kennedy (2017) outlined a meaning-making model to describe process by which growth is achieved. In their model, persons have global meanings – overarching beliefs, goals, and purposes. These global meanings are similar to Janoff-Bulman's (1992) concept of an assumptive world. There are also situational meanings – the application of global meaning to a particular event. If an event's situational meaning violates global meaning, distress ensues. Individuals are motivated to reduce this distress by two means: they can reappraise the specific event to come in line with the global meaning, or they can revise the global meaning to match the situational event.

As an example, consider a woman whose adult child died in a car accident. Her global meanings of "life is fair," "children outlive their parents," and "I am a good mother" were violated by the tragedy. Trying to determine how such a meaningless event had occurred would be accompanied by distress, anxiety, anger, and depression. However, meaning-making (see Altmaier, 2017) eventually allows for an improved situational meaning ("I am a better person after having experienced the loss of a child") and changed global meaning ("I will transform this event into a commitment to improving the lives of others").

Achterhof et al. (2018) surveyed over 400 persons who survived a severe earthquake at two time points after the earthquake. Relevant to considerations of the effects of trauma, there was an overall decrease in distress between the first and second time point. Also, most participants reported post-traumatic growth at the second time point. Higher distress at the first time point was related to higher post-traumatic growth at the second, suggesting that the growth process was a coping response to the trauma, thus supporting a process model.

Distinctions between growth as a process or an outcome are relevant to building models to be empirically tested, but are not as relevant to clinicians working to foster growth in their clients. More important is the universality of the phenomenon of growth. Many persons have documented post-traumatic growth, from events as wide ranging as terrorist attacks (McCormack & McKellar, 2015); assault, including sexual assault (Elderton, Berry, & Chan, 2017); military combat (Park et al., 2017); health problems, both chronic and life threatening (Wang et al., 2017); and the suicide of a child (Moore, Cerel, & Jobes, 2015).

Some traumas are experienced on a communal scale, as is the case with war-related combat and migration. Uy and Okubo (2018) conducted a study of Cambodian community leaders who survived the Khmer Rouge genocide and then became refugees to the United States. Post-traumatic growth was clear in the participants' narratives, and had occurred in domains that had been previously established, namely appreciation of life, and gratitude for having it; establishing new priorities; valuing family and other interpersonal relationships. However, for these leaders, growth also occurred in a collective way through their continued leadership in their cultural communities in the United States. That continuance occurred, partly, because of the willingness of the leaders to disclose their experiences and experience support in their communities.

There has been an explosion of research into post-traumatic growth, its occurrence in a wide variety of traumas and among a range of people. Illustrative of this growth, there were over 1500 papers published since 2010 on the topic, many attempting to establish predictors of growth based on the nature of the traumatic event, the characteristics of the person and his or her social context, and the process itself. Post-traumatic growth promises to be an important application of a strengths-based approach to assisting persons after trauma.

Summary

Positive psychology has served to reinvigorate the commitment of researchers and scholars to understanding the good life even within life's difficulties and traumas. Contributions have included the scientific study of human strengths, their definition and their operation. The meaning of the good life, explaining flourishing as a life style, and clarity in understanding happiness and well-being are among recent research findings. All clients, especially those experiencing significant impairments in their everyday lives, benefit from these advances.

It is also evident that theory and research, along with clinical work, has established the importance of an active process after trauma using resources from personal strengths to re-establish a pattern of growth and engagement. Part of that active process, as will be evident in the following chapters on specific personal strengths, is the ongoing struggle to remain engaged with difficult emotional and cognitive experiences that reveal the effect of the trauma on everyday life. Positive processes are a key means by which the traumatized person re-engages in life.

References

Achterhof, R., Dorahy, M. J., Rowlands, A., Renouf, C., Britt, E., & Carter, J. D. (2018). Predictors of posttraumatic growth 10–11 months after a fatal earthquake. *Psychological Trauma: Theory, Research, Practice, and Policy, 10*, 208–215.

Altmaier, E. M. (Ed.), (2017). *Reconstructing meaning after trauma: Theory, research, and practice*. New York, NY: Elsevier.

Beidel, D. C., Bulik, C. M., & Stanley, M. A. (2014). *Abnormal psychology* (3rd ed.). Upper Saddle River, NJ: Pearson Education, Inc.

Boehm, J. K., & Lyubomirsky, S. (2009). The promise of sustainable happiness. In S. J. Lopez, & C. R. Snyder (Eds.), *The Oxford handbook of positive psychology* (2nd ed., pp. 667–677). New York, NY: Oxford University Press.

Bonanno, G. A. (2004). Loss, trauma, and human resilience: Have we underestimated the human capacity to thrive after extremely aversive events? *American Psychologist, 59*, 20–28.

Case, A., & Deaton, A. (March 23–24, 2017). *Mortality and morbidity in the 21st century*. Brookings Papers on Economic Activity. Downloaded from https://www.brookings.edu/wp-content/uploads/2017/03/6_casedeaton.pdf.

Charry, E. T. (2011). Positive theology: An exploration in theological psychology and positive psychology. *Journal of Psychology and Christianity, 30*, 283–292.

Charry, E. T., & Kosits, R. D. (2017). Christian theology and positive psychology: An exchange of gifts. *Journal of Positive Psychology, 12*, 468–479.

Christopher, J. S., & Hickinbottom, S. (2008). Positive psychology, ethnocentrism, and the disguised ideology of individualism. *Theory & Psychology*, *18*, 563–589.

Diener, E. (1984). Subjective well-being. *Psychological Bulletin*, *93*, 542–575.

Diener, E., & Lucas, R. E. (1999). Personality and subjective well-being. In D. Kahneman, E. Diener, & N. Schwarz (Eds.), *Well-being: The foundations of hedonic psychology* (pp. 213–229). New York, NY: Russell Sage Foundation.

Duckworth, A. L., Steen, T. A., & Seligman, M. E. P. (2005). Positive psychology in clinical practice. *Annual Reviews of Clinical Psychology*, *1*, 629–651.

Elderton, A., Berry, A., & Chan, C. (2017). A systematic review of posttraumatic growth in survivors of interpersonal violence in adulthood. *Trauma, Violence, & Abuse*, *18*, 223–236.

Gallup News. (2017). *State of the American Workplace*. Available from http://news.gallup.com/reports/199961/state-american-workplace-report-2017.aspx.

Garrett, L. E., Spreitzer, G. M., & Bacevice, P. A. (2017). Co-constructing a sense of community at work: The emergence of community in coworking spaces. *Organization Studies*, *38*, 821–842.

Huta, V., & Ryan, R. M. (2010). Pursuing pleasure or virtue: The differential and overlapping well-being benefits of hedonic and eudaimonic motives. *Journal of Happiness Studies*, *11*, 735–762.

Janoff-Bulman, R. (1992). *Shattered assumptions: Toward a new psychology of trauma*. New York, NY: Free Press.

Joseph, S., & Linley, P. A. (Eds.), (2008). *Trauma, recovery, and growth: Positive psychological perspectives on posttraumatic stress*. New York, NY: John Wiley & Sons, Inc.

Krakauer, M. (2018). The effect of an adjunctive positive psychology intervention with a focus on gratitude and communication oriented strategies on relationship satisfaction and positive interactions in distressed couples: A preliminary investigation. *Dissertation Abstracts International*, Section B: 79 (2-B(E)).

Li, T., Liu, T., Han, J., Zhang, M., Li, Z., Zhu, Q., & Wang, A. (2018). The relationship among resilience, rumination, and posttraumatic growth in hemodialysis patients in North China. *Psychology, Health & Medicine*, *23*, 442–453.

Linley, P. A., & Joseph, S. (2005). The human capacity for growth through adversity. *American Psychologist*, *60*, 262–264.

Linley, P. A., & Leontiev, D. (2009). Multiple dimensions of the good life: Introducing international and interdisciplinary perspectives. *The Journal of Positive Psychology*, *4*, 257–259.

Lopez, S. J., & Snyder, C. R. (Eds.), (2009). *Oxford handbook of positive psychology* (2nd ed.). New York, NY: Oxford University Press.

McCormack, L., & McKellar, L. (2015). Adaptive growth following terrorism: Vigilance and anger as facilitators of posttraumatic growth in the aftermath of the Bali bombings. *Traumatology*, *21*, 71–81.

McMahan, E. A., Choi, I., Kwon, Y., Choi, J., Fuller, J., & Josh, P. (2016). Some implications of believing that happiness involves the absence of pain: Negative hedonic beliefs exacerbate the effects of stress on well-being. *Journal of Happiness Studies*, *17*, 2569–2593.

Moore, M. M., Cerel, J., & Jobes, D. A. (2015). Fruits of trauma? Posttraumatic growth among suicide-bereaved parents. *Crisis: The Journal of Crisis Intervention and Suicide Prevention*, *36*, 241–248.

Myers, D. G., & Diener, E. (1995). Who is happy? *Psychological Science*, *6*, 10–19.

Neff, K. (2003). Self-compassion: An alternative conceptualization of a healthy attitude toward oneself. *Self and Identity*, *2*, 85–101.

Park, C. L., & Kennedy, M. C. (2017). Meaning violation and restoration following trauma: Conceptual overview and clinical implications. In E. M. Altmaier (Ed.), *Reconstructing meaning after trauma* (pp. 17–27). New York, NY: Elsevier.

Park, C. L., Smith, P. H., Lee, S. Y., Mazure, C. M., McKee, S. A., & Hoff, R. (2017). Positive and negative religious/spiritual coping and combat exposure as predictors of posttraumatic stress and perceived growth in Iraq and Afghanistan veterans. *Psychology of Religion and Spirituality, 8*, 13–20.

Parsons, F. (1909). *Choosing a vocation*. Boston, MA: Houghton, Mifflin and Co.

Peterson, C., & Park, N. (2009). Classifying and measuring strengths of character. In S. J. Lopez, & C. R. Snyder (Eds.), *Oxford handbook of positive psychology* (2nd ed., pp. 25–33). New York, NY: Oxford University Press.

Peterson, C., Park, N., & Seligman, M. E. P. (2005). Orientations to happiness and life satisfaction: The full life versus the empty life. *Journal of Happiness Studies, 6*, 25–41.

Peterson, C., & Seligman, M. E. P. (2004). *Character strengths and virtues: A handbook and classification*. Washington, DC: American Psychological Association, and New York, NY: Oxford University Press.

Ryff, C. D. (1989). Happiness is everything or is it? Explorations on the meaning of psychological well-being. *Journal of Personality and Social Psychology, 57*, 1069–1081.

Ryff, C. D., & Keyes, C. L. M. (1995). The structure of psychological well-being revisited. *Journal of Personality and Social Psychology, 69*, 719–727.

Schnitker, S. A., & Emmons, R. A. (2017). The psychology of virtue: Integrating positive psychology and the psychology of religion. [Special issue]. *Psychology of Religion and Spirituality, 9*(3).

Seligman, M. E. P. (2002). *Authentic happiness: Using the new positive psychology to realize your potential for lasting fulfillment*. New York, NY: Free Press.

Seligman, M.E.P. (February 24, 2017). *The PERMA model: Your scientific theory of happiness*. Downloaded from https://positivepsychologyprogram.com/perma-model/.

Seligman, M. E. P., & Csikszentmihalyi, M. (2000). Positive psychology: An introduction. *American Psychologist, 55*, 5–14.

Seligowski, A. V., Miron, L. R., & Orcutt, H. K. (2015). Relations among self-compassion, PTSD symptoms, and psychological health in a trauma-exposed sample. *Mindfulness, 6*, 1033–1041.

Tallman, B.A. (2011). *Anticipating posttraumatic growth from cancer: A patient and collateral perspective*. (Doctoral dissertation). Retrieved from https://search.proquest.com/pqdtlocal1005838/docview/902757942/fulltextPDF/B8643B44F04E4B89PQ/1?accountid = 14663.

Tallman, B. A., Altmaier, E. M., & Garcia, C. (2007). Finding benefit from cancer. *Journal of Counseling Psychology, 54*, 481–487.

Tedeschi, R. G., & Calhoun, L. G. (1995). *Trauma and transformation: Growing in the aftermath of suffering*. Thousand Oaks, CA: Sage Publications.

Tedeschi, R. G., & Calhoun, L. G. (1996). The Posttraumatic Growth Inventory: Measuring the positive legacy of trauma. *Journal of Traumatic Stress, 9*, 455–471.

Tedeschi, R. G., & Calhoun, L. G. (2004). Posttraumatic growth: Conceptual foundations and empirical evidence. *Psychological Inquiry, 15*, 1–18.

Terrill, A. L., Reblin, M., MacKenzie, J. J., Cardell, B., Einerson, J., Berg, C. A., ... Richards, L. (2018). Development of a novel positive psychology-based intervention for couples post-stroke. *Rehabilitation Psychology, 63*, 43–54.

Trompetter, H. R., Kleine, E., & de Bohlmeijer, E. T. (2017). Why does positive mental health buffer against psychopathology? An exploratory study on self-compassion as a resilience mechanism and adaptive emotion regulation strategy. *Cognitive Therapy and Research*, *41*, 459–468.

Uy, K. K., & Okubo, Y. (2018). Reassembling a shattered life: A study of posttraumatic growth in displaced Cambodian community leaders. *Asian American Journal of Psychology*, *9*, 47–61.

Van der Kolk, B. A. (2014). *The body keeps the score: Brain, mind, and body in the healing of trauma*. New York, NY: Viking.

Wang, A. W., Chang, C., Chen, S., Chen, D., Fan, F., Carver, C. S., & Hsu, W. (2017). Buffering and direct effect of posttraumatic growth in predicting distress following cancer. *Health Psychology*, *36*, 549–555.

Wierzbicka, A. (2009). What makes a good life? A cross-linguistic and cross-cultural perspective. *The Journal of Positive Psychology*, *4*, 260–272.

Witmer, L. (1913). Children with mental defects distinguished from mentally defective children. *The Psychological Clinic*, *7*, 173–181.

Resources for clinicians and clients

Algoe, S. B., & Haidt, J. (2009). Witnessing excellent in action: The "other-praising" emotions of elevation, gratitude, and admiration. *Journal of Positive Psychology*, *4*, 105–127.

Keyes, C. L. M., & Haidt, J. (2002). *Flourishing: Positive psychology and the life well-lived*. Washington, DC: American Psychological Association.

Ryff, C. D., & Singer, B. H. (2008). Know thyself and become what you are: A eudaimonic approach to psychological well-being. *Journal of Happiness Studies*, *9*, 13–39.

Seligman, M. E. P. (2018). *The hope circuit: A psychologist's journey from helplessness to optimism*. New York, NY: Hachette Book Group.

Sin, N. L., & Lyubomirsky, S. (2009). Enhancing well-being and alleviating depressive symptoms with positive psychology interventions: A practice-friendly meta-analysis. *Journal of Clinical Psychology*, *65*, 467–487.

Tedeschi, R. G., & Moore, B. A. (2016). *The posttraumatic growth workbook: Coming through trauma wiser, stronger, and more resilient*. Oakland, CA: New Harbinger Publications.

VIA Survey of Character Strengths. Viacharacter.org//www/Character-Strengths-Survey.

Hope

3

Hope is a central pivot in human existence. Consider the great distance between "hopeless" and "hopeful": hopeful people anticipate and expect desired things to happen, while hopeless people are resigned to a fate outside of their control. Hope is paradoxical, in that if hope exists, so must despair (Lynch, 1962). Both hope and despair have a long tradition of discussion in philosophy and religion as well as in the human sciences. However, as Rand and Cheavens (2009) note, these discussions were often one-sided, and hope was either "heralded or maligned."

Positive psychology reinvigorated the scientific study of hope by recognizing its essential role in adaptation, and scholars contributed to its investigation by proposing hope as having two distinct characteristics. First, hope was defined as a plan or intent rather than a wish or a desire. Second, hope was centered in cognitions as opposed to emotions. In positive psychology, hope has more to do with thinking, rather than feeling, although feelings are a contributor. As early as 1959, Menninger defined hope this way: "Unconcerned with the ambiguity of past experience, hope implies process; it is an adventure, a going forward, a confident search" (p. 484).

This chapter builds on the work of positive psychology regarding hope, using a definitional structure established by Eaves, Nichter, and Ritenbaugh (2016). In their research on hope among adults with chronic pain, multiple interviews over time yielded individual narratives about future expectations. These narratives were then categorized into distinct, dynamic meanings of hope: cognitive, existential, faith, and embodied phenomena. In the cognitive experience, participants described hope as realistic, factoring practical considerations into the judgment; or as wishful, essentially the maintenance of positive illusions (see Taylor, 1983). Existential hope was indicated by the presence or the absence of a general hopefulness that was unrelated to a specific outcome or goal. Faith-based hope was aligned with a religious or spiritual tradition and with faith in science and medicine. Embodied hope was grounded in assumptions about the body itself, for example, that people have innate healing abilities that can and will operate.

This chapter considers hope as a positive process after trauma. Theory and research pertinent to hope is presented. How hope creates ways for traumatized persons to better live "in the world" is detailed. In this chapter, too, are Kimberly's responses to the following definition and questions:

Hope definition

A certain type of thinking, where the individual has desired goals, believes that pathways are available to meet those goals, and actively intends to pursue those

Promoting Positive Processes after Trauma. DOI: https://doi.org/10.1016/B978-0-12-811975-4.00003-4
Copyright © 2019 Elsevier Inc. and Kimberly Gleason. All rights reserved.

pathways; hope relates to emotions as valued goals are reached (positive emotions) or as unsurmountable barriers exist (negative emotions); hope reflects related constructs of optimism and self-efficacy.

Hope questions

Hope is presumed to be learned during childhood, within experiences of cause and effect. Do you, looking back, see that you had hope during your childhood?
How did that hope express itself?
Looking back, how did hope help and/or hinder your response during and after trauma?
For the hope you did have, how did you come to have it?
What were similarities among events that increased your hope, and what were similarities among events that decreased your hope?
What might help others increase hope in their own efforts to set and achieve valued personal goals?

Defining hope

Hope as a cognitive process

The participants in the study of Eaves et al. (2016) first described hope as an intellectual or cognitive process and their narratives revealed certain themes. First, hope was realistic, or practical. Second, hope was collective, in that individuals saw their experience fitting within a larger community of participants. Third, hope was wishful, understanding that certain illusions maintain hope in "dire" circumstances. This type of hope was also cognitive in that it was grounded in expectations.

The conceptualization of hope by researchers and clinicians in positive psychology, as mentioned earlier, focused on hope as a cognitive process, the interaction of personal goals, pathways (means to reach those goals), and agency (energy that is available to be directed toward the achievement of those goals along the pathways (Snyder, 2002; Snyder, Rand, & Sigmon, 2002; Rand & Cheavens, 2009)). The term "goals" applies to a variety of purposes, ranging from the fleeting to the long-lasting. Goals may be positive or negative. Positive goals are goals of approach, of attaining a desired outcome, or of maintaining that outcome over time. Negative goals are goals of avoidance, trying to stop, or delay an unwanted outcome before it occurs.

The second concept is pathways, actions to achieve the goals. As with goals, pathways vary on many dimensions. Getting ourselves from one point to another in the goal attainment process may rely on one carefully developed pathway that is followed doggedly, or on several pathways that are tried and discarded based on the experienced success or failure. Additionally, people differ in their approach to create these pathways. For some, the awareness of possible obstacles might be included in pathway development; for others, the knowledge that the goal will involve extended effort might factor into planning.

The last concept is agency, self-referential thinking that links the goal and the pathway in occurrence. Agency is the intention to act, the belief that actions are possible, and the energy to act. As with goals and pathways, individuals also differ in their agency. Some people are narrowly agentic; they have confidence that certain goals and pathways are possible, but not all. Others are globally agentic; they believe that they can achieve what they set their minds and actions to achieve, and those beliefs and that confidence extends across a range of life domains.

Hope as an existential process

Existential hope was a second type of hope in the narratives provided by patients in the study of Eaves et al. (2016), defined as a hope unattached to a specific goal or outcome. This hope focused on the possibilities of a good outcome in general, one not defined by a cure of the chronic pain per se, but rather by renewed ability to live with whatever outcome occurred. This type of hope defended against despair, in that participants relied on this hope to avoid giving up.

Hope in this existential sense is similar to another construct considered in positive psychology, that of optimism. *Optimism* is a generalized expectation for a good outcome, regardless of the problem, while pessimism is a generalized expectation for a bad outcome. Within positive psychology (see Carver, Scheier, & Segerstrom, 2010), optimism is a broad version of confidence pertaining to life in general. Since optimism relates to the expectation of a good outcome, it would be expected that people who are high on optimism persist in the face of challenges, engage in pursuit of goals, and work harder at obtaining and maintaining personal resources.

Research supports the correlation of optimism with direct problem-solving. Nes and Segerstrom (2006), for example, conducted a *meta-analysis* (a study of published studies) that noted the positive relationship of optimism with approach coping and problem-focused coping, and a negative relationship of optimism with problem avoidance and emotion avoidance. More optimistic people used methods of approach and problem-solving, while less optimistic people were more likely to avoid difficult problems and distressing emotions.

Are hope and optimism the same construct or overlapping? Fowler, Weber, Klappa, and Miller (2017) used confirmatory factor analysis to compare varying models of their relationship. Based on data from over 400 participants, hope and optimism were revealed to be similar and different. The similarity is that both constructs represent individuals' positive expectations for their own futures. The difference is that hope relates to individual actions: I can achieve that desired outcome based on my own actions. Optimism considers positive outcomes as due to a variety of factors, including luck and the actions of others in addition to personal actions.

Hope as a faith-driven process

Faith was present in hope among the patient narratives (Eaves et al., 2016) in two ways. The first was faith in the science underlying increasingly more effective medical treatments. More pertinent to this chapter is the second, faith grounded in a religious tradition. Most religious traditions encourage hope as a component of faith. Within Christianity, such an encouragement is clear in the Biblical Book of Hebrews, where the author describes hope as "being certain of things we cannot see" (Hebrews 11:1, Phillips). Research evidence (Stanton, Danoff-Burg, & Huggins, 2002) supports "turning to religion" as important for persons needing hope: in their study of 70 women with breast cancer, women lower in hope who used more religious forms of coping (e.g., "I put my trust in God") demonstrated improved mood and adjustment.

Faith-based hope operates in particular ways. For example, Ciarrocchi, Dy-Liacco, and Deneke (2008) surveyed over 200 adults who endorsed a variety of faith traditions concerning what variables predicted their hope. Among those adults, one's perceived personal relationship with a deity, level of spiritual commitment, and ability to create meaning in difficult circumstances (meaning-making) positively predicted hope in contrast to other variables that did not predict hope, such as personal identification as a "religious person" and attendance at religious services.

The importance of a personal commitment to faith was clear in a large-scale survey conducted by Bertold and Ruch (2014). In their survey, over 20,000 participants of many religious affiliations and persons of no religious affiliation were compared on character strengths (positive resources), including hope. Religious people who reported practicing their religion reported more hope than respondents who had no religious affiliation and respondents who had a religious affiliation but did not practice their religion.

Hope as an embodied process

The last aspect of hope in patient narratives was an embodied hope, a hope based in people's assumptions about their own bodies. Those assumptions centered on beliefs in processes possessed by their own bodies that would promote healing. Having hope itself was also thought to be a powerful addition to the process of healing, even if the means by which this addition worked were unknown.

The power of expectation is the basis for the use of placebos in medicine and other human treatment. A *placebo* is a presumably inert substance or intervention believed by the patient to have been effective; thus the patient expectations of cure are the mechanism of cure. While placebo response has been studied widely, the means by which this outcome occurs are not identified. Recent research (e.g., Howe, Goyer, & Crum, 2017; Thibault & Raz, 2017) highlights roles of personal expectation, motivation, and vigilance to information provided by the environment.

Here are Kimberly's thoughts regarding the positive process of hope in her life both during and after trauma.

> Looking back at my childhood, I did have hope. Knowing what I know now as an adult, I believe it would more accurately be defined as faith. Having faith that even though today may not be a good day, tomorrow can be better. I have always had something inside of me telling me that as long as I do what I know to be right, then "things will work out." Sometimes it's hard to stop all the clutter and noise, to get to where you know what is right. But I do believe

you can. You have to shut off the noise, and figure this out. For me, I would often force myself to look at my immediate thought before all doubt set in.

When I stop to really dig in and try to define or figure out where this hope came from, it's difficult. It's as though it was always there. And I would be willing to go so far as to say that some are born with it. What happens to this innate faith depends what life experiences a child has, and what people a child has in life, and probably some personality predispositions as well. If a child grows up in a horrible environment and does not have anyone to help point them in a positive direction or help nurture a faith in humanity, that hope may start to dim. If a child is brought up in a home with wonderful people and experiences, they may blossom and shine. But I do believe that some are just born with a deeper hope, even when faced with several adverse conditions such as sexual abuse, divorce, and a father with health problems who eventually died at a young age.

I experienced some pretty difficult circumstances, even before the sexual abuse started. My parents divorced when I was only four and a half years old. And my dad had his first heart attack when I was three. This was big for me and for my development when I experienced the power of something bigger than myself. I could not see my dad's heart, nor could I see this attack. But it showed me that things exist even though we cannot see them or even really understand them. And even bigger than this, my dad did not die. He lived. But how was I to know that a heart attack was not going to happen again? How was I going to rest my head without concern of my dad dying tomorrow?

You may think I was only three and did not think of such things at the time, but I'm sure I did, especially seeing how my own boys' brains work and process information at a young age. Although children may not express their worries in a way we can understand, that does not mean that they are not trying to make sense of their world. My dad went on to have several more heart attacks and two major open-heart surgeries. What enables you to cope with such adult problems as a young child? Hope. Some may have the luxury of turning their minds off and are able to do what they're told when adults advise, "don't worry about that." But for me, it took something more. It took having faith in something bigger than myself to ease this worry. And again, I did not always define this hope as a child, and especially didn't understand it, but I still had faith.

Looking back through my life, I believe it is the hard times that taught me to have hope, which I later came to recognize as faith. When you face challenges that are so great, and are completely outside of your control, you could drive yourself crazy with worry and concern. I believe it is beneficial to step back and assess what control you have over the situation that is causing you concern. For those things outside your control, you still have a choice of what to do with them. For me, my faith taught me and allowed me to believe in a better tomorrow, and hold onto hope that some day things would be better. And maybe, just maybe some day I might have a better understanding of everything. For the things you can control, I believe it is best to face the things you can head-on, no matter how difficult they are. The sooner you face them, the sooner they begin to dissipate. And I know this sounds weird from the girl who never said anything about her abuse for 20 years, but consider this as speaking from experience: Freedom cannot be attained until you face it.

Hope after trauma

How does hope occur after trauma? It seems contradictory to expect that positive expectations for the future can co-exist with the degree of disconnection experienced by persons after trauma. As noted by Herman (1992), trauma destroys the victim's basic trust in the fabric of assumptions that tie us to the world: that the world has meaning and order, that the world is a safe place, that we are persons of dignity and worth. Trust and hope are interconnected, in that hope is predicated on expectations of a future that is trustworthy, that is, that the future will operate according to assumptions about life.

Hope represents the work of recovery. *Recovery* is an ambiguous term: is recovery merely the absence of those symptoms associated with the "diagnosis" of the condition from which recovery was required? Our own personal experience, as well as extensive research, suggests that in the same way that health is more than the absence of illness, recovery is more than the absence of symptoms. Recovery is a process with several characteristics: it is individual and unique, it can happen without a "cure," it is a difficult struggle, it takes trial and error, and it is not linear but quite irregular.

Tasks involved in recovery were outlined by Leamy, Bird, Le Boutillier, Williams, and Slade (2011). The very first task is that recovery requires hope and optimism about the future. Recovery demands a belief that change can happen, that there is a new possible self, and that hope exists even in the presence of that which speaks against change. Recovery will be rooted in meaning, a topic of Chapter 7. Recovery also demands a new personal identity clear of shame, stigma, and betrayal.

Recent research using qualitative designs have contributed to our understanding of the necessary preconditions and co-occurring contexts for hope to be identified and utilized in recovery. As an example, Srivastava (2015) conducted interviews with 22 women who had experienced a trauma in young adulthood; these traumas included physical assault, sexual abuse, and traumatic bereavement. Grounded theory analyses of the narrative data revealed the factors which influenced whether hope and trust were effective in recovery. These factors were a social network of family and other support persons, time for solitude and reflection, experiencing strengths in oneself that countered the presence of fear and anger, and willingness to tolerate and even embrace the very real struggle to obtain meaning.

Another qualitative study of trauma survivors (Egger, 2018), in this case victims of sexual trafficking, revealed a similar dialectic or contrast between recovery work that goes on alone, and recovery work that includes the support of others. Qualitative themes derived from the interview-obtained narratives revealed that hope worked in aloneness through introspection, desire for change, willingness to have flexibility in circumstances, and positive self-appraisal. Hope worked in connection, through attachment providing both instrumental support and emotional support.

Another relevant construct for hope after trauma is personal theories. *Personal theories* (see Martin, 1994) are organized ways in which we have expectations for and perceive our experiences. These theories depend heavily on our past experience, our memories. Trauma memories create personal theories that emphasize fear, distress, and distrust. These theories, then, organize experience around a need for safety and for avoidance of any threatening stimulus. Personal theories are maintained partially through avoidance: not experiencing a potential threat leads to relief, but also to failure to learn that the event is actually safe.

Interaction with others, especially those high in empathic understanding and trustworthiness, can create personal change through several means. A study of the fostering of hope within a group of similarly situated persons (adults with chronic pain; Larsen, King, Stege, & Egeli, 2015) revealed that participants experienced four means by which their hope was influenced by the group. The first was awareness, hearing new perspectives and seeing strengths among others. The second was comparison, being inspired by others and also seeing oneself as having made progress compared to others. Communion was the third theme, receiving support from others and serving as a resource for others. Last was connection, knowing that one had shared hope in "banding together" and also shared difficulty.

Kimberly discusses how she experienced hope during her recovery.

> My hope expressed itself by always knowing deep inside that despite everything, tomorrow is another day bringing another opportunity. Often when things would get difficult or I would feel confused about things, I would write in a journal. I am a huge proponent for writing to purge feelings from being bottled up inside. But also for me, writing brought a way to think things through. Things would be a little clearer and make more sense once down on paper. Obviously, life didn't change in the time it took me to write, but rather, my outlook would refocus. It allowed me to understand what I am able to control and what is beyond my control. For those things outside of my control, I work on letting them go. Through my own life experience I have learned that you can either allow things to eat you up inside or you can work on realizing it is beyond your control and to let go. There is no magic process for this, but for me, realizing which category something is in helps you begin to process through it and move forward.
>
> I believe that my hope gave me the ability to buckle down and embrace the heartache. It allowed me the ability to be okay even though I didn't feel okay in a particular moment. It allowed me to feel awful and have bad days, because I knew they were just that. Temporary. They were bad days, and tomorrow brings a new opportunity. My hope has also brought me to the realization in life that there really is no point in asking "why?" when bad things happen. There is no answer that will suffice or make you feel better anyway. Nothing will take any deep pain away by knowing why. The better question is "what?" Instead of dwelling on why, which won't get me anywhere anyway, I focus on all the "what" questions. What does this mean going forward? What can I do with this? What am I supposed to learn from this?

Promoting hope

Although trauma reduces the availability of hope, hope can be reaffirmed. Levi, Liechtentritt, and Savaya (2012) studied Israeli soldiers with chronic post-traumatic stress disorder, all of whom experienced a trauma during their military service (e.g., being taken prisoner). The results of this study revealed several important aspects of the "clash" between hope and trauma. First, although all participants described having no hope during the trauma, they all reported that re-establishing hope was one of their first responses after trauma. Second, in order to be hopeful again, participants used others as a source of hope, especially noting that external sources of hope complemented their own budding internal hope. Last, the soldiers all realized that to fully overcome their trauma, part of their recovery was the work it took them to initiate and sustain hope.

Lopez et al. (2004) defined certain strategies useful for promoting hope. The first are hope finding and hope reminding, processes similar to benefit finding and meaning-making, where exploration and narration of stories can identify the presence of hope. Hope bonding is the use of others as sources of hope, particularly as the stories of others create a more available hope. Hope enhancing is the use of short-term goals and their achievements to promote the setting of more complex goals and to create strategies for their attainment.

Hope is also found by the active debunking of vulnerability myths (Brown, 2012). In her book, *Daring Greatly*, Brown analyzed narrative responses she obtained in her research to determine how people move out of fear and toward courage. She identified several beliefs that impeded that movement: believing that being vulnerable was equivalent to being weak, believing that one can "opt out" of experiencing vulnerability in life, believing that vulnerability meant exposing one's complete self indiscriminately, and believing that being vulnerable meant life without social support and connections.

In contrast to those vulnerability beliefs, building hope through being open to oneself and experience means living with courage, purpose, and connection: those elements that define hope within a positive psychology framework. This lifestyle is what Brown terms "daring greatly," practicing gratitude for small ordinary moments, having self-compassion, and cultivating our spirits. In this text, we will return to many of those themes in the chapters ahead.

Hope can also be promoted indirectly. The use of art, music, and poetry can speak to the survivor in evocative language. An example of this indirect promotion was a study of 29 women with breast cancer (Daboui, Janbabai, & Moradi, 2018) who participated in weekly sessions organized around poetry. The authors reported significant increase in hope among the women, and noted that the group connecting to each other around mystical themes was a potent influence of improvement.

Kimberly discusses how she created and used hope in her trauma response.

> I do believe there are things someone can do to help develop a sense of hope. Taking the time to stop and get to know yourself can really help to keep you grounded and to allow yourself to see a better tomorrow. It's important to know what we like and what we don't like, what makes us happy or sad, and what makes us anxious. Knowing what makes you feel different ways can help you identify how you need to alter your perspective when faced with challenges. I went through a huge period of self-discovery as part of my recovery from my trauma, both the initial trauma of abuse as well as the trauma of exposure.
>
> It is during this self-discovery process that you begin to make sense of the traumatic event, to identify it, and to realize its impact on you. You start to understand yourself better and begin to know why things that may seem to make no sense at all, make complete sense in context of your traumatic experience. There is power is being able to identify that a particular behavior or thought process is a result of what happened to you, and not a part of your natural character.
>
> One of the most powerful things we can do is to connect with other survivors. We may carry shame and guilt, unknowingly, over something that we believe makes us weird and different. And it may be something so small, yet it's something we would not dare share with another. However, something special happens when you can connect with another survivor and learn that "you're not the only weirdo." Suddenly we find freedom when we know that the behavior is a result of something that happened to us, and not simply us. Freedom is found, and shame and guilt are shed.

I think it's important to be willing to try new things. If we always utilize the same tools, we cannot expect to get different results. I would place post-it notes on my bathroom mirror, so I would see them first thing in the morning and last thing before bed. I used words of encouragement as well as reminders to keep my thoughts straight when faced with challenges that may distort my views.

Though this practice is not for everyone, I found tattoos beneficial for me when it comes to critical reminders in my life. A couple months after my dad died, at age 19, I got the Chinese symbols for dream, respect, and faith. "Follow your dreams" means to keep pushing and don't stop when you come to an obstacle. Expect that nothing worth having comes without difficulty. "Respect yourself" is a reminder to value myself, and know that I am worth more than the many failed coping mechanisms I had tried as a teen. And "never lose faith" means to keep believing that something better is to come, even when we don't understand things and find ourselves with complete heartache.

When you get in a funk, it helps to stop and be grateful. Refocus on what you have in your life, what is good, and who is important to you. There were days that I would force myself to write down three things for which I was grateful before I could go to bed. When your mind starts down a dark path, and you don't want to get sucked down further, you have to be willing to help yourself first. Now as part of our bedtime routine with our children, we each write down our top five things we're thankful for from our day. We want to teach our children how important it is to maintain a positive mindset and to exemplify for them the power of showing gratitude first.

And for those things you cannot control, I believe you still have to manage your emotions. You still need to allow yourself time to process through things, and to allow your heart the opportunity to do what it needs to do to heal. But ultimately, you have to realize your lack of control but believe that tomorrow will work out and be better. I know this does not mean that things will work out how or when you want them to, but regardless, they will work out. One thing I've learned for sure is life rarely unfolds on our ideal timeline, but yet it makes sense as we look back and see how it has all come together to bring us to the current moment in time and helped to shape us into who we are.

Summary

Hope is an initial strength needing to be promoted after trauma. Trauma, after all else, speaks against future hope, and its resolution necessitates a restoration of hope. Within the positive psychology framework, hope positions us for additional progress. The virtue of courage speaks to the movement toward a goal, persisting through obstacles, and showing bravery. The virtue of transcendence includes connections to meaningful and spiritual aspects of the university through hope and gratitude. And as hope speaks through the experiences of others, we build the virtue of humanity.

References

Bertold, A., & Ruch, W. (2014). Satisfaction with life and character strengths of non-religious and religious people: It's practicing one's religion that makes the difference. *Frontiers in Psychology*, *5*, 876, 14 August, 2014.

Brown, B. (2012). *Daring greatly: How the courage to be vulnerable transforms the way we live, love, parent and lead*. New York, NY: Penguin Books.

Carver, C. S., Scheier, M. F., & Segerstrom, S. C. (2010). Optimism. *Clinical Psychology Review, 30*, 879–889.

Ciarrocchi, J. W., Dy-Liacco, G. S., & Deneke, E. (2008). Gods or rituals? Relational faith, spiritual discontent, and religious practices as predictors of hope and optimism. *The Journal of Positive Psychology, 3*, 120–136.

Daboui, P., Janbabai, G., & Moradi, S. (2018). Hope and mood improvement in women with breast cancer using group poetry therapy: A questionnaire-based before-after study. *Journal of Poetry Therapy*. Available from https://doi.org/10.1080.08893675.2018.1467822.

Eaves, E. R., Nichter, M., & Ritenbaugh, C. (2016). Ways of hoping: Navigating the paradox of hope and despair in chronic pain. *Culture, Medicine, and Psychiatry, 40*, 35–58.

Egger, A. (2018). Human sex trafficking: How sex trafficking victims and survivors experience hope and resilience. *Dissertation Abstracts International, 78*. (11-B(E)).

Fowler, D. R., Weber, E. N., Klappa, S. P., & Miller, S. A. (2017). Replicating future orientation: Investigating the constructs of hope and optimism and their subscales through replication and expansion. *Personality and Individual Differences, 116*, 22–28.

Herman, J. (1992). *Trauma and recovery*. New York, NY: Basic Books.

Howe, L. C., Goyer, J. P., & Crum, A. J. (2017). Harnessing the placebo effect: Exploring the influence of physician characteristics on the placebo response. *Health Psychology, 36*, 1074–1082.

Larsen, D. J., King, R. L., Stege, R., & Egeli, N. A. (2015). Hope in a strengths-based group activity for individuals with chronic pain. *Counselling Psychology Quarterly, 28*, 175–199.

Leamy, M., Bird, V., Le Boutillier, C., Williams, J., & Slade, M. (2011). Conceptual framework for personal recovery in mental health: A systematic review and narrative synthesis. *The British Journal of Psychiatry, 199*, 445–452.

Levi, O., Liechtentritt, R., & Savaya, R. (2012). Posttraumatic stress disorder patients' experiences of hope. *Qualitative Health Research, 22*, 1672–1684.

Lopez, S. J., Snyder, C. R., Magyar-Moe, J. L., Edwards, L. M., Pedrotti, J. T., Janowski, K., ... Pressgove, C. (2004). Strategies for accentuating hope. In P. A. Linley, & S. Joseph (Eds.), *Positive psychology in practice* (pp. 388–404). Hoboken, NJ: Wiley.

Lynch, W. F. (1962). *Images of hope: Imagination as healer of the hopeless*. Baltimore, MD: Helicon Press.

Martin, J. (1994). *The construction and understanding of psychotherapeutic change: Conversations, memories, and theories*. New York, NY: Columbia University Press.

Menninger, K. (1959). The academic lecture: Hope. *The American Journal of Psychiatry, 116*, 481–491.

Nes, L. S., & Segerstrom, S. C. (2006). Dispositional optimism and coping: A meta-analytic review. *Personality and Social Psychology Review, 10*, 235–251.

Rand, K. L., & Cheavens, J. S. (2009). Hope theory. In S. J. Lopez, & C. R. Snyder (Eds.), *The Oxford handbook of positive psychology* (pp. 323–333). New York, NY: Oxford University Press.

Snyder, C. R. (2002). Hope theory: Rainbows in the mind. *Psychological Inquiry, 13*, 249–275.

Snyder, C. R., Rand, K. L., & Sigmon, D. R. (2002). Hope theory: A member of the positive psychology family. In C. R. Snyder, & S. J. Lopez (Eds.), *Handbook of positive psychology* (pp. 257–276). New York, NY: Oxford University Press.

Srivastava, M. (2015). Trauma, trust and hope among women: A qualitative study. *Psychological Studies*, *60*, 170–184.
Stanton, A. L., Danoff-Burg, S., & Huggins, M. E. (2002). The first year after breast cancer diagnosis: Hope and coping strategies as predictors of adjustment. *Psycho-Oncology*, *11*, 93–102.
Taylor, S. E. (1983). Adjustment to threatening events: A theory of cognitive adaptation. *American Psychologist*, *38*, 1161–1173.
Thibault, R. T., & Raz, A. (2017). The psychology of neurofeedback: Clinical intervention even if applied placebo. *American Psychologist*, *72*, 679–688.
Van der Kolk, B. A. (1997). Traumatic memories. In P. S. Appelbaum, L. A. Uyehara, & M. R. Elin (Eds.), *Trauma and memory: Clinical and legal controversies* (pp. 243–260). New York, NY: Oxford University Press.
Westburg, N. G. (2001). Hope in older women: The importance of past and current relationships. *Journal of Social and Clinical Psychology*, *20*, 354–365.

Resources for clinicians and clients

Brown, B. (2012). *Daring greatly: How the courage to be vulnerable transforms the way we live, love, parent and lead.* New York, NY: Penguin Books.
Clark, D. A. (2014). *The mood repair toolkit: Proven strategies to prevent the blues from turning into depression.* New York, NY: Guilford Press.
Gallagher, M. W., & Lopez, S. J. (2018). *The Oxford handbook of hope.* New York, NY: Oxford University Press.
Hays, P. A. (2014). *Creating well-being: Four steps to a happier, healthier life.* Washington, DC: American Psychological Association.
Lamott, A. (2018). *Almost everything: Notes on hope.* New York, NY: Penguin Group.
Lopez, S. L. (2014). *Making hope happen: Create the future you want for yourself and others.* New York, NY: Simon & Schuster.
McDermott, D., & Snyder, C. R. (2000). *The great big book of hope: Help your children achieve their dreams.* Oakland, CA: New Harbinger Publications.
Snyder, C. R. (2003). *Psychology of hope: You can get there from here.* New York, NY: The Free Press.

Positive emotionality

4

A marker of well-being, which is a central concept of positive psychology, is happiness. Happiness is usually defined as the presence of positive emotions, the absence of negative emotions, and the presence of life satisfaction. Although life satisfaction might sound like a marker that is nonemotional in nature, research (see Schimmack & Oishi, 2005) suggests that our assessments of life satisfaction are more affected by immediate contextual factors, such as emotional states, rather than by a careful judgment across multiple life domains. Therefore, emotions are critically influential in our sense of happiness and in our well-being. We know that life after trauma has much to do with negative emotions, both their experience and their avoidance. However, those many negative emotions do not drive out the possibility of also experiencing happiness through positive emotions after trauma.

One difficulty in examining the role of emotions is that relevant terms have been confused over time and now denote overlapping meanings, most notably the terms "affect," "emotion," and "mood." While many distinctions exist, a classification scheme proposed by Ekkekakis (2012) is helpful and will be used in this text. In that scheme, *affect* is the accessible, general, even primitive experience of feeling. Examples of affect are pleasure, displeasure, vigor, and fatigue. *Emotion* is the experience of affect joined with cognitive appraisal of the eliciting stimulus, with behavioral expression, and with concurrent physiological changes. Examples of emotions are fear and anger. *Mood*, in contrast, is a diffuse and global feeling not linked in time with a cause. Examples are a good mood or an irritable mood ("getting up on the wrong side of the bed," or being "out of sorts").

This chapter explores two aspects of emotions especially significant for the traumatized person – first, that the experience of positive emotions has a facilitating effect on adaptation, and second, that the awareness and expression of both positive and negative emotions is beneficial. In this chapter, too, are Kimberly's responses to the following definition and questions:

Emotionality definition

The frequent experience of positive emotions that produce optimal functioning in varying circumstances by broadening possible responses and building personal resources; the expression, rather than avoidance, of emotions in general; the effective use of personal emotions to improve thinking and responding.

Promoting Positive Processes after Trauma. DOI: https://doi.org/10.1016/B978-0-12-811975-4.00004-6
Copyright © 2019 Elsevier Inc. and Kimberly Gleason. All rights reserved.

Positive emotionality questions

Looking back, what messages did you receive as a child about emotions, both positive and negative?

Were you discouraged from having emotions in general, or particular emotions?

What analogy would you use to describe how your emotions affected or did not affect you during trauma?

What changes have occurred in your experiencing of emotions, positive and/or negative, after trauma?

Sometimes emotions can teach us, can give us information about ourselves. How have you experienced that phenomenon?

What might help someone else accept and use their own emotions to improve their adaptation to traumatic circumstances?

The role of positive emotions

Positive emotions have two distinct significant roles to play in changing the individual's trauma-dominated life. The first role is that positive emotions occur with and stimulate different coping responses than negative emotions. We know that negative emotions, especially fear, shame, sadness, and avoidance, are normal responses to traumatic events. However, these normal responses tend to drive coping responses of denial, distortion, and withdrawal. Those *avoidance coping* responses, in turn, continue and even increase negative emotions of fear, sadness, and distress. Holahan, Moos, Holahan, Brennan, and Schutte (2005) examined avoidance coping among 1000 adults over a 10-year time period and documented that use of avoidance coping was associated with more life stress after 4 years, and it was responsible for increased depression.

In contrast, Folkman (1997) drew attention to how meaning-focused coping generates positive emotions, and those positive emotions sustain coping over time. Meaning-focused coping is a collective term for coping responses associated with searching for and finding meaning: positive reappraisal, goal-directed problem-focused coping, spiritual beliefs and practices, and infusing events with positive meaning. An initial benefit of meaning-focused coping is that individuals approach, rather than avoid, the traumatic experience and its elements in order to create meaning with their coping responses.

When positive emotions are generated from meaning-focused coping, they further assist the traumatized individual in several ways. First, simply by experiencing positivity, the individual has a respite from difficulty and distress. Second, as coping produces positivity, the individual begins to develop a self-image of efficacy rather than failure. As confidence in oneself to continue coping increases, the appraisal of the event changes from "overwhelming" to "challenging," creating a positive feedback loop. Third, specific strategies in meaning-focused coping increase a sense of connectedness to others, whether those others are in the same circumstances or in the personal social world.

The second role for positive emotions in changing a post-trauma life is that they create a positive spiral. Fredrickson (1998, 2001) defined how positive emotions, such as joy and contentment, create momentum to reverse the trauma–isolation–distress sequence. Her model is the *broaden-and-build theory* of positive emotions. The first step, broaden, is the expansion of thought–action linkages. As an example, the experience of "curious interest" broadens the individual as he or she is motivated to explore the environment, learns new information, and experiences different events. In a confirmatory study (Fredrickson & Branigan, 2005) where participants enumerated possible actions to be taken after a laboratory-induced condition, joy and contentment resulted in a larger number of actions than fear and anger, and also more actions than a neutral condition. The authors noted that broadening occurred as the individual's scope of attention was widened and as thought–action linkages were pursued.

The second step is build, the notion that personal resources – increased physical, intellectual, and social capacity – are built over time as a result of positive emotions and their thought–action linkages. By creating awareness of positive experiences, new actions and new responses follow. These new actions and responses, in turn, create increased flexibility that over time results in additional personal resources. A study of midlife working adults (Fredrickson, Cohn, Coffey, Pek, & Finkel, 2008), for example, revealed that people who received an intervention to help them cultivate self caring for both mind and body reported increases in nine distinct positive emotions (e.g., contentment, joy). These gains in positive emotions then increased their life satisfaction.

Both positive and negative emotions appear to be self-perpetuating to some degree (see Burns et al., 2008), meaning that they influence cognitive, behavioral, and physical processes that maximize their recurrence. Negative emotions, such as sadness, can lead to rumination, which results in less cognitive flexibility and more tendency to see the world as negative, resulting in more loss and sadness, a situation that is a downward spiral. In contrast, positive emotions create exposure to positive situations, influence the occurrence of other positive concepts such as resilience, and accumulate in a positive way, an upward spiral.

The broaden-and-build model should not be understood to suggest that "pursuing happiness" is a helpful goal by itself. In fact, research suggests the opposite. Mauss, Tamir, Anderson, and Savino (2011) studied community living adults regarding whether the degree to which they valued happiness was associated with their own happiness and well-being. In this study, a greater value placed on happiness was associated with less well-being and higher depression for participants who were under conditions of low life stress. Additional research (McGuirk, Kuppens, Kingston, & Bastian, 2018) has revealed that rumination over an experience of failure in a context where happiness is especially salient resulted in lowered well-being.

Rather, as Catalino, Algoe, and Fredrickson (2014) demonstrated, the pursuit of *positivity* ("My major decisions in life are influenced by how much I might experience positive emotions") is associated with different outcomes than the pursuit of happiness ("If I don't feel happy, maybe there is something wrong with me"). In predicting well-being or depression, life satisfaction was associated with prioritizing positivity while depression was associated with pursuit of happiness. Importantly, individuals who prioritized positivity experienced more positive emotions, and reported more social resources (e.g., self-compassion, resilience).

The experience of positive emotions, therefore, is a significant resource for increasing living in the present among persons after trauma.

> *Positive emotions, although transient, have lasting consequences; they build durable personal resources whose accrual triggers further positive emotions, leading to self-sustaining upward spirals of well-being. Conversely, when negative emotions accrete into downward spirals of defensive behavior, focus on threat, and feelings of inefficacy, these self-destructive, vicious cycles can lead to impoverished life experiences.*
>
> *Garland et al. (2010), p. 860*

Kimberly experienced a deficit of positive emotions, both as a child and as an adult. In her narrative, it is possible to discern a downward spiral during childhood, but an upward spiral in her recent experience.

> I don't recall specifically discussing emotions [during my childhood], as far as which ones were okay and which ones were not. I did, however, pick up messages, whether they were intentional or not, from my mom's family. Some of my greatest frustrations growing up came from the way emotions were handled, or rather, not handled. I always felt nobody could ever be direct and say what they wanted, or how they felt. Yet later they would be upset and have hurt feelings because their needs were not met. You were just supposed to know, but nobody could ever say.
>
> At the same time that no one was open about their feelings, you also were not allowed to have feelings of your own. There was this unspoken sense of needing to agree with the family. If you had different thoughts and feelings, it was not acceptable, and you were made to feel bad. The most difficult part of all of this dynamic was it had become so much the way things were that I'm not sure if anyone recognized it. But as a child I saw it from the beginning and was always confused by it and didn't like it.
>
> I remember feeling a sense of responsibility for others' happiness. I constantly had to do things because others wanted me to or because it was expected of me. I was not taught to make decisions and choices based on what is best for me, and what I wanted, but rather to think of what everyone else wanted and expected of me. And I don't mean in the sense that, as a child, there are many things we must do that we don't want to. It was more than that. It was constant family expectations, of lunch every Saturday and Sunday at noon. Or traveling four and a half hours in the car with the whole family to go mow my great-grandparents' yard every other weekend growing up. It was as though we always had to do what was expected of us, and what we should do, and nobody ever stopped to think about if it was something we really wanted to do.
>
> My husband has increased my ability to communicate my emotions and my desires. He has this phrase which I have come to love, which sounds overly simplistic but is completely true. "Say what you mean and mean what you say." He would remind me of this phrase sometimes during our early arguments. If I didn't want him to do something but I said, "I don't care," and then later was upset with him for making a choice, he would remind me that it was not fair to expect him to know what I meant or what I expected if I didn't say it. I realize it may be more difficult and may require you to be more vulnerable to say how you really feel but I do believe

it is important to stretch yourself and learn how to do this. This phrase has come to be one that I so frequently remind myself of and have shared with others. "Say what you mean and mean what you say."

Looking back, I can see that my ability to put my emotions in a box was both detrimental and beneficial for me. I was most affected by the way my abuse stripped me of my ability to be intimate. I don't mean this in the sexual sense, though this was affected as well, but more in the way to truly draw close to someone, to know and be known by them, to love and be loved by them. It is difficult for me to believe that the other person will be there, and not leave or hurt me. I always have my guard up and am acutely aware that at any moment the relationship may turn a different direction or disappear completely.

Sometimes this need to rationalize things keeps me from freely feeling my emotions. I was recently trying to work through some emotions and was making a list of all the things that my stepdad, Mike, took from me. I started with innocence, trust, destroying the relationship with my dad, intimacy, etc. As I was making this list, I did not get very far before my thoughts were interrupted, "but this has made you who you are today" and then later "but this has brought you many opportunities to help others now." My rational thoughts were interrupting my ability to freely feel my emotions. I do believe though this is the lesser of two evils, because it is this quality of not allowing myself to spiral downward that I also believe helps me to demonstrate resilience.

When you first come face to face with your sexual abuse you have so many emotions. You cannot even believe it yourself. Then in addition to the denial, you feel guilt and shame, you feel unworthy of people's time, you assume people won't believe you, you wonder what you could have done to stop it, you blame yourself, and you wish it would all go away. Sometimes you may even feel as though the world would be better if you would go away. Though I experienced this trauma and all the emotions of that little girl I once was, I had the massive benefit of having an adult brain to process through it all. This adult brain is what always reminded me that if I could just hold onto the truth, nobody could take the truth from me.

I had already experienced my own family not believing me and knew that some of them would never come to terms with the harsh reality of Mike's evil ways. So long as I lived and made choices consistent with the truth of Mike's devious ways, nobody could take that from me. They could deny it, they could blame me, they could cry entrapment, but they could not take the truth from me. The truth is my stepdad molested me 20 years back, later got arrested after placing an ad on Craigslist for a daddy-daughter fantasy, and later decided to commit suicide to avoid facing his sociopathic world of lies crumbling around him.

The positive role of all emotions

The aftermath of trauma is often feeling overwhelmed by negative emotions: fear, depression, hopelessness, and anger. Managing those emotions (i.e., not being overcome by them) is a goal in the process of becoming a "post-traumatic self" (see Wilson, 2006). However, emotional management is typically thought of as reducing or suppressing the intensity of emotions, or methods to reframe or alter a situation to reduce its emotional stimulus power. In traditional coping assessment (i.e., COPE; Carver, Scheier, & Weintraub, 1989), scales that measure coping methods for emotion management include mental disengagement, denial, and humor. The implication is that strong emotional experience is dysfunctional and maladaptive, and that effective coping reduces the experience of these negative emotions.

In contrast to that traditional view is the research by Stanton (see Stanton, 2011; Stanton & Low, 2012) that documents benefits that can be achieved by two specific types of *emotional approach*: emotional processing and emotional expression. Emotional approach is movement toward, rather than away from, emotions, including distressing emotions. Emotional processing is active attempts to acknowledge, explore, and understand emotions. Emotional expression is verbal and nonverbal communication of emotions. Examples of emotional processing would be recognizing that feelings are valid and important, and taking time to label and understand actual feelings. Examples of emotional expression would be journaling and verbal venting.

Persons with chronic health conditions often report a history of trauma and adversity, along with emotional unawareness and emotional avoidance. In recent research, two such patient groups received training directed at helping them recognize that their avoidance of emotions was a stressor in and of itself. The training focused on their being able to experience and express emotions, and engage in direct communication with others. Thakur et al. (2016) studied adults with irritable bowel syndrome. Patients who learned emotional awareness and expression experienced improvement in their health symptoms and their quality of life. A second study with adults who presented with medically unexplained symptoms (Ziadni et al., 2018) resulted in similar findings. Patients who received training in emotional awareness and expression reported reduced pain, fewer sleep problems, and improved psychological function.

As mentioned earlier, emotional experience depends partly on cognitive appraisal. In fact, research suggests that we have *emotional schemas* (see Leahy, 2002). These schemas are personal models of the function of emotions. One such schema is ventilation: if I have emotions, the more I express them, the better off I am. Such a person would experience emotions, attend to them, believe these emotions are normal, and accept and express them. Another schema is avoidance: all emotions are frightening and should be avoided. Such a person would experience emotions, notice them, but then actively avoid them through self-numbing and dissociation. A third schema is that emotions can be good or bad, but bad emotions are problematic. This third person would experience emotions, attend to them, and then ruminate over them: should they be experienced? Is there social consensus that they are appropriate? If the emotion created guilt or worry, the individual would avoid situations that elicit these particular emotions or blame their occurrence on the actions of others.

Here are Kimberly's thoughts on emotional awareness and experience.

> Experiencing my emotions, especially as things were exposed, has changed a lot. I have learned to be more patient with myself and give myself grace. I allow myself to really feel things, whether they make sense in the moment or not. I own my emotions, knowing they are mine, and cannot be wrong or taken from me. It is good to feel whatever emotions I have, and I need to work through them; right, wrong, or indifferent. I know this does not mean I can act upon them however I want, but I am entitled to feel whatever emotions come. And honestly, it's better to feel things as they come than to try to numb them or stuff them away.
>
> I have also experienced the power of sharing stories and emotions with other survivors. There is power in talking with another survivor that "gets it" and "knows" what you have been through. There are things you carry and feel guilt or shame about, and then when you

speak to another survivor, you learn it's normal for us to experience or feel. It is helpful to learn that it is not some character flaw or something wrong with you, but rather a result of the trauma you experienced. And sometimes, it is as easy as another survivor acknowledging the feeling, so we can more easily accept it as something that makes us different and move forward. I very much believe an important part of the healing journey is seeking to better understand your trauma and the impact it has had on your life. This is not to make excuses, but how can you hope to heal without first understanding?

I also believe we have a choice to make about emotions. You can simply step over, and walk around emotions. You can scoop them up and shove them away in the closet. Or, you can make the choice to work through your emotions, choosing to "let go" of some and to reframe and keep others. I have made the choice to sort through my memories, reframe, and reorganize things. This is not an easy task at all. It takes a lot of time and patience. I have felt many emotions that don't make sense, and I then step back and sort through what exactly I'm really feeling. I have found that anger tends to be a secondary emotion for me. When I feel angry, it is usually because I really am feeling hurt or disappointment. Sometimes it takes a while to step back and uncover what you're really feeling. But I do believe it is worth the effort. You are worth the effort. One thing I have learned is you cannot move past an emotion until you have allowed yourself to be fully immersed and feel the magnitude of its impact.

Promoting positive emotionality

There are practical ways to learn to approach emotions, both positive emotions and negative emotions. For example, a model of emotional intelligence (see Salovey, Mayer, & Caruso, 2002) specifies four skills of effectively using emotions. The first skill is "emotional perception and expression;" this term pertains to accurately identifying emotion in oneself and in others. The second is "emotional facilitation of thought"; more difficult tasks in this skill are using emotions and thinking in reflective, mutually enhancing, ways – for example, using emotional states to improve problem-solving. The third is "emotional understanding," an ability to understand complex emotions, primary and secondary emotions, and relationships among emotions. The fourth is "emotional management," a term which denotes openness to emotions rather than avoidance of them.

All of these skills rely on accurately recognizing emotions in oneself, and accepting their presence. Rather than avoidance, an orientation toward self-compassion is needed. *Self-compassion* (see Neff, 2003) is literally offering compassion to the self. That self-compassion is being open to one's own suffering, offering a nonjudgmental understanding of one's own pain, and seeing one's own experience as fitting in the larger human experience. Self-compassion is not weakness or passivity; rather being compassionate to one's self provides the same type of emotional safety that being compassionate to another provides. Additionally, self-compassion is not pity: self-pity usually denotes being identified with one's own suffering, being over absorbed in feelings. Self-compassion promotes a balanced awareness of self.

A recent study of over 300 adults from a general population (Trompetter, deKleine, & Bohlmeijer, 2016) revealed that individuals who exercised the strength of self-compassion were able to use that as a resource during negative emotions. It seems that self-compassion served as a route toward promoting emotional expression and acceptance. This relationship was also demonstrated in a study of 121 older adults (Homan, 2016), where self-compassion additionally served as a buffer between health concerns and depression.

The focus of this text is on promoting positive processes among clients to further the goal of their living in the present, of being open to their experience. There are challenges to being open to emotions, and a common fear among trauma survivors is being overtaken by their emotions. But emotional regulation does not mean emotional suppression or avoidance. Keeping a daily journal of emotions can help clients identify if they are approaching or avoiding difficult emotions. Helping clients think about the influence of their culture on their emotional awareness and expression can lead to insights about the messages clients internalized from their history. Last, narrative methods help clients "retell" their stories. As Liu (2013) described, writing trauma stories in a community writing workshop was significantly helpful to veterans.

Kimberly talks about ways she became more aware of and expressive of her emotions.

> I learned to talk myself through things, using the technique I describe as "Being your own best friend." As I would feel things, I would stop and ask myself what I would say to my best friend, or if the feelings would make sense provided the situation someone described them to me. I can face discomfort and sit with negative emotions, if I can justify it as normal or expected. Sometimes you just have to know you're going to have a bad or difficult day, but provided your circumstance, it's normal. And sometimes you feel fine one minute and awful the next, but given the amount of chaos you're trying to process through, that is to be expected. I believe it is completely okay to have bad days, and sometimes even bad weeks.
>
> I believe writing is a powerful tool in learning about your own emotions. One reason is that writing is a way to unlock a door to thoughts and feelings from inside us. Another reason is it allows you the opportunity to read about yourself in a third person way. Sometimes we get so overwhelmed by our emotions and cannot sort through them. But when we step back and are able to read through them, it makes sense. Writing can provide you the distance that permits clarity.
>
> Sometimes if I feel I have drifted too far from my emotions and feel out of touch, but yet something is troubling me and I know I need to work through it, I use photos to reconnect. There is something with actually seeing yourself as a child, or seeing your perpetrator in the context of a "stepdad" yet also finally acknowledging all the evil he perpetrated. Another helpful tool is to find a photo of yourself from the time of your abuse. If this is not possible, find a photo of a child close to this age. After writing a letter to get your story on paper, read it while looking at this photo. It is easy to hold ourselves to a higher standard and be hard on ourselves. It is much harder to blame yourself when you can visibly see the child you actually were. I believe it would be very difficult to look at the child inside that photo without a great deal of empathy and compassion.
>
> Again, with the idea of "Becoming your own best friend", writing a letter can make this easier. You can write a letter explaining things, and get your feelings on paper. Then if you step back and read it as though it's from a friend, you can gain insight and understanding. We often respond to others with compassion, understanding, and empathy, but we tell ourselves to toughen up and deal with it, or that we should be "over it" by now. Allowing ourselves this insight into our own circumstance may allow us to give ourselves more grace and patience. You're allowed to have a bad day. It is better to feel things as they come rather than try to stuff them away, or turn to other unhealthy coping mechanisms.

Summary

It might be an exaggeration to say that "emotions are our friends" when those emotions overwhelm everyday life. Life after trauma often means that emotions feel hard, overwhelming, and dark. From the perspective of positive psychology, however, emotions have a critical influence on being more in-the-world for trauma survivors. Positive emotions are caused by certain types of coping, and generate more positive emotions and sustained coping. Emotional approach, instead of emotional avoidance, can facilitate adaptive functioning even in stress-filled contexts. As noted by Cohn and Fredrickson (2009), "Positive emotions contribute to both the pleasurable life and the good life... Positive emotions allow us to sample the rewards of the future in the present" (p. 21).

Self-compassion is a mechanism by which strengths begin to mitigate against effects of trauma. In terms of emotionality, self-compassionate people tend to report more positive emotionality and lower distress (see MacBeth & Gumley, 2012). Further, Leary, Tate, Adams, Allen, and Hancock (2007) documented through a series of studies that self-compassion predicts emotional and cognitive effects of negative personal experiences. Self-compassion, therefore, encourages both positive emotions and approach of all emotions, an orientation toward self-awareness and self-caring.

References

Burns, A. B., Brown, J. S., Sachs-Ericsson, N., Plant, E. A., Curtis, J. T., Fredrickson, B. L., & Joiner, T. E. (2008). Upward spirals of positive emotion and coping: Replication, extension, and initial exploration of neurochemical substrates. *Personality and Individual Differences*, *44*, 360–370.

Carver, C. S., Scheier, M. F., & Weintraub, J. K. (1989). Assessing coping strategies: A theoretically based approach. *Journal of Personality and Social Psychology*, *56*, 267–283.

Catalino, L. I., Algoe, S. B., & Fredrickson, B. L. (2014). Prioritizing positivity: An effective approach to pursuing happiness? *Emotion*, *6*, 1155–1161.

Cohn, M. A., & Fredrickson, B. L. (2009). Positive emotions. In S. J. Lopez, & C. R. Snyder (Eds.), *The Oxford handbook of positive psychology* (2nd ed., pp. 13–24). New York, NY: Oxford University Press.

Ekkekakis, P. (2012). Affect, mood, and emotion. In G. Tenenbaum, R. C. Eklund, & A. Kamata (Eds.), *Measurement in sport and exercise psychology* (pp. 321–332). Champaign, IL: Human Kinetics.

Folkman, S. (1997). Positive psychological states and coping with severe stress. *Social Science and Medicine*, *45*, 1207–1221.

Fredrickson, B. L. (1998). What good are positive emotions? *Review of General Psychology*, *2*, 300–319.

Fredrickson, B. L. (2001). The role of positive emotions in positive psychology: The broaden-and-build theory of positive emotions. *American Psychologist*, *56*, 218–226.

Fredrickson, B. L., & Branigan, C. (2005). Positive emotions broaden the scope of attention and thought-action repertoires. *Cognition and Emotion*, *19*, 313–332.

Fredrickson, B. L., Cohn, M. A., Coffey, K. A., Pek, J., & Finkel, S. M. (2008). Open hearts build open lives: Positive emotions, induced through loving-kindness meditation, build consequential personal resources. *Journal of Personality and Social Psychology, 95*, 1045–1062.

Garland, E. L., Fredrickson, B., Kring, A. M., Johnson, D. P., Meyer, P. S., & Penn, D. L. (2010). Upward spirals of positive emotions counter downward spirals of negativity: Insights from the broaden-and-build theory and affective neuroscience on the treatment of emotion dysfunctions and deficits in psychopathology. *Clinical Psychology Review, 30*, 849–864.

Holahan, C. J., Moos, R. H., Holahan, C. K., Brennan, P. L., & Schutte, K. K. (2005). Stress generation, avoidance coping, and depressive symptoms: A 10-year model. *Journal of Consulting and Clinical Psychology, 73*, 658–666.

Homan, K. J. (2016). Self-compassion and psychological well-being in older adults. *Journal of Adult Development, 23*, 111–119.

Leahy, R. L. (2002). A model of emotional schemas. *Cognitive and Behavioral Practice, 9* (3), 177–190.

Leary, M. R., Tate, E. B., Adams, C. E., Allen, A. B., & Hancock, J. (2007). Self-compassion and reactions to unpleasant self-relevant events: The implications of treating oneself kindly. *Journal of Personality and Social Psychology, 92*, 887–904.

Liu, R. Z. (2013). "The things they carried": Unpacking trauma scripts inside a community writing workshop. *Counselling Psychology Quarterly, 26*, 55–71.

MacBeth, A., & Gumley, A. (2012). Exploring compassion: A meta-analysis of the association between self-compassion and psychopathology. *Clinical Psychology Review, 32*, 545–552.

Mauss, I. B., Tamir, M., Anderson, C. L., & Savino, N. S. (2011). Can seeking happiness make people unhappy? Paradoxical effects of valuing happiness. *Emotion, 11*, 807–815.

McGuirk, L., Kuppens, P., Kingston, R., & Bastian, B. (2018). Does a culture of happiness increase rumination over failure? *Emotion, 18*, 755–764.

Neff, K. (2003). Self-compassion: An alternative conceptualization of a healthy attitude toward oneself. *Self and Identity, 2*, 85–101.

Salovey, P., Mayer, J. D., & Caruso, D. (2002). The positive psychology of emotional intelligence. In C. R. Snyder, & S. Lopez (Eds.), *Handbook of positive psychology* (pp. 159–171). New York, NY: Oxford University Press.

Schimmack, U., & Oishi, S. (2005). The influence of chronically and temporarily accessible information on life satisfaction judgments. *Journal of Personality and Social Psychology, 89*, 395–406.

Stanton, A. L. (2011). Regulating emotions during stressful experiences: The adaptive utility of coping through emotional approach. In S. Folkman (Ed.), *The Oxford handbook of stress, health, and coping* (pp. 369–386). New York, NY: Oxford University Press.

Stanton, A. L., & Low, C. A. (2012). Expressing emotions in stressful contexts: Benefits, moderators, and mechanisms. *Current Directions in Psychological Science, 21*, 124–128.

Thakur, E. R., Holmes, H. J., Lockhart, N. A., Carty, J. N., Ziadni, M. S., Doherty, H. K., … Lumley, M. A. (2016). Emotional awareness and expression training improves irritable bowel syndrome: A randomized controlled trial. *Neurogastroenterology & Motility, 29*, e13143.

Trompetter, H. R., deKleine, E., & Bohlmeijer, E. T. (2016). Why does positive mental health buffer against psychopathology? An exploratory study on self-compassion as a resilience mechanism and adaptive emotion regulation strategy. *Cognitive Therapy and Research, 41*, 459–468.

Wilson, J. P. (Ed.), (2006). *The posttraumatic self: Restoring meaning and wholeness to personality*. New York, NY: Routledge.

Ziadni, M. S., Carty, J. N., Doherty, H. K., Porcerelli, J. H., Rapport, L. J., Schubiner, H., & Lumley, M. A. (2018). A life-stress, emotional awareness, and expression interview for primary care patients with medically unexplained symptoms: A randomized controlled trial. *Health Psychology*, *37*, 282–290.

Resources for clinicians and clients

Fredrickson, B. (2009). *Positivity: Top-notch research reveals the upward spiral that will change your life*. New York, NY: Crown Publishers.

Fredrickson, B. (2013). *Love 2.0: Finding happiness and health in moments of connection*. New York, NY: Penguin Group.

Greenspan, M. (2003). *Healing through the dark emotions: The wisdom of grief, fear, and despair*. Boston, MA: Shambhala Publications.

Gruber, J., & Moskowitz, J. T. (Eds.), (2014). *Positive emotion: Integrating the light sides and the dark sides*. New York, NY: Oxford University Press.

Hasson, G. (2014). *Emotional intelligence: Managing emotions to make a positive impact on your life and career*. New York, NY: Wiley.

Tugade, M. M., Shiota, M. N., & Kirby, L. D. (Eds.), (2014). *Handbook of positive emotions*. New York, NY: Guilford Press.

Resilience

5

Although much of the research discussed in this text was conducted on adults, we know that trauma equally occurs in the lives of children. Further, for children, the extreme stressors of trauma are significantly compounded by children's dependence on adults and on larger community systems for protection. Research reveals that trauma during childhood creates both immediate and long-term problems through its impact on developing systems. While childhood trauma occurs in community-experienced events, such as natural disasters or school shootings, it is also the case that childhood trauma occurs in the home, through abuse, neglect, and violence. The term *Adverse Childhood Experiences* (ACE) is used to denote these events and includes the following: abuse (physical, emotional, sexual), neglect (physical, emotional), violence (parental, familial), conflict (parental, divorce), and separation (incarceration of parent or caregiver).

The United States government, through agencies such as the Centers for Disease Control and Prevention and the Substance Abuse and Mental Health Services Administration, has increasingly focused on these childhood events and their prevention as a significant public health concern. This attention is warranted since research (see <https://www.cdc.gov/violenceprevention/acestudy>) has shown that ACEs are common (60% of the original sample reported 1 or more ACE events and 6%, 4 or more). Additionally, experiencing ACE events increases adult risk of mental and substance use disorders, suicide and depression, high-risk sexual behaviors, and other health problems (e.g., sleep disorders) (see Felitti et al. (1998) for original study)

Historically, psychologists focused their clinical and scholarly attention on children who experienced traumas in attempts to understand how some children did not display the expected negative effects from trauma while other children did. As early as World War II, clinicians (e.g., Freud & Burlingham, 1943) described children exposed to bombings and other combat horrors. Children who were with their mothers or other caregivers during the war environment did not appear to be as traumatized as children who were separated, possibly because their parents' presence became a protective factor. Later in the century, psychologists (e.g., Werner & Smith, 1992) noted that certain children who should be "at risk" after enduring childhood traumas were actually exhibiting adaptive development. The term that came to be used for these children was *resilience*, "positive adaptation during or following significant adversity or risk" (Masten, Cutuli, Herbers, & Reed, 2009; p. 118).

Resilience is a strength present during development. However, resilience also applies to adults and to their functioning after trauma. In this chapter, theory and research concerning resilience among children as well as adults is presented. How resilience seems to buffer trauma and its effects is a primary interest, and how

Promoting Positive Processes after Trauma. DOI: https://doi.org/10.1016/B978-0-12-811975-4.00005-8
Copyright © 2019 Elsevier Inc. and Kimberly Gleason. All rights reserved.

clinicians can foster clients' recognition and enhancement of this strength is also considered. In this chapter, too, are Kimberly's responses to the following definition and questions:

Resilience definition

An individual's capability to adapt to significant adversity that would typically challenge physical and mental health; resilience is influenced by factors within the child (such as temperament, positive outlook), factors in the family and other close relationships (such as family climate, positive attachments), and by factors in the community (such as public safety, support for cultural traditions).

Resilience questions

Do you, looking back, see that you had resilience during your trauma?
Where was that resilience in you, and where was it in interactions with others?
Looking back, how did resilience help and/or hinder your response?
For the resilience you did have, how did you come to have it?
Were there specific life experiences that you believe made you "more resilient?"
What might help someone be more resilient during or after trauma?

In resilience discussions, *risk* is the term for the likelihood of a negative outcome given the context, whether that context is physically problematic (such as violence), emotionally problematic (such as neglect or abuse), or socially problematic (such as poverty or deficits in family support). *Cumulative risk* is the effect of several risk factors, either occurring at the same time or accumulating over time. For example, having an absent parent, living in poverty, and experiencing sexual abuse is a high cumulative risk for a child or adolescent. *Protective factors* are variables that are empirically associated with a positive outcome in spite of risk or cumulative risk. *Assets* are factors that create a likelihood of positive outcome whether or not risk is present.

Lopez, Pedrotti, and Snyder (2015) provide examples of protective factors and assets that clarify the differences between them. Protective factors occur within the child, within the family and other relationships, and within the community. Examples of the first are self-regulation skills, positive temperament, and problem-solving skills. Examples of the second are close relationships that are positive, warm, and affirming. And examples of the last are involvement in prosocial organizations such as church or Boys and Girls Clubs. In contrast, assets improve everyone's well-being, whether or not children are at risk; assets include safe neighborhoods, access to relevant community services, and effective schools.

Defining resilience

Resilience is considered to be present when positive adaptation in the midst of crisis is present, but how is it more specifically defined? One way to explain resilience is to identify certain people who have demonstrated resilience, who differed from others in the same circumstances by rising above or by "bouncing back," and then identify the characteristics that seemed to be influential to their adaptation. Werner and Smith (1982) followed all children born in 1955 on a Hawaiian island into adulthood, studying them at ages 1, 2, 10, 18 and 32. Some of these children were deemed "at risk" because of stressors in their family environment (e.g., parental alcoholism); of these at risk children, about two-third demonstrated learning problems or behavior problems in childhood and adolescence. However, adaptation increased between adolescence and adulthood; when studied at age 32, a smaller percentage (approximately 18%) had adult life problems, including criminal records and chronic mental health issues.

What were the protective factors that allowed most of the "at risk" sample to achieve successful adaptation in adulthood? Werner and Smith (1992) identified four clusters of protective factors. Cluster 1 were characteristics of the individuals themselves, such as an easy temperament. Cluster 2 were parental characteristics, such as warm caregiving styles. Cluster 3 was the presence of supportive adults outside of the immediate family, such as youth leaders, teachers, and grandparents. Cluster 4 were skills and abilities developed by the individuals over time which led to creating and pursuing realistic vocational plans.

Werner (1993) summarized this important research as follows:

> *When we examined the links between protective factors within the individual and outside sources of support or of stress, we noted a certain continuity that appeared in the life courses of the high-risk men and women who successfully overcame a variety of childhood adversities. Their individual dispositions led them to select or construct environments that, in turn, reinforced and sustained their active, outgoing dispositions and rewarded their competencies (p. 508).*

A second approach to defining resilience is empirical, studying a large group of people, only some of whom have experienced risk, and statistically comparing various categories of people. In an effort to understand resilience factors that promoted successful aging among adults, Jeste et al. (2013) studied 1006 community living adults ages 50–99 years old. An extensive assessment process measured physical, cognitive, and psychological factors and self-rated "successful aging." The authors used self ratings of successful aging in addition to objective determinants employed by other researchers, such as cognitive deficits, disease, and depression. Self ratings allow older adults to include attitudinal factors in addition to objective factors.

Among the participants, successful aging was predicted by greater resilience; resilience was found to be having the strengths of hardiness and persistence (see Campbell-Sills & Stein, 2007). *Hardiness* is the ability to cope with change, including difficulties such as illness, unexpected events, and negative emotions; *persistence* is giving one's best effort to achieve important personal goals even in the face of obstacles and roadblocks. Bonanno (2004) also considered the concept of resilience in adults, and noted that multiple, and sometimes unexpected or unlikely mechanisms, are present in adult resilience. He also argued for the resilience influence of hardiness, self-enhancement, and positive emotions. Hardiness has been previously defined. Self-enhancement is the use of positive views of the self. Positive emotions are means to reduce distress and create more resources.

Kimberly did not consider herself as having resilience. But from her narrative, it is apparent that many expected negative sequelae from her childhood trauma did not occur in her adult life, likely because she had both hardiness and persistence as well as the presence of protective factors.

> Looking back, initially, I didn't see resilience. I saw that I did what I had to do, and really, had no options. To me, giving up wasn't an option and I knew rolling on the floor in a fetal position wouldn't solve anything. Now people tell me how resilient I am all the time, but I'm just starting to understand and see what they see.
>
> My dad had his first heart attack when I was three years old, and I remember picking him up from the hospital. He continued to have heart attacks as I grew up, and had a couple major open-heart surgeries, sometimes repairing five vessels at a time. It feels as though I grew up with my dad dying. I learned very early that life isn't fair, and you shouldn't expect it to be. And it's not our job to "make sense" of the world or the things that happen around us. But rather to adjust, and trust that at some point when we look back on what occurred, it may make a little more sense later.
>
> I believe when I was younger, I did what I needed to do for survival. There are very few people who I believe I could have told [about the abuse] who would have believed me and acted to help me. The piece a lot of people don't understand is when a child tells you something like that, it requires immediate action. The list is very short of individuals who would have believed me immediately and also had the wherewithal to know what steps needed to be taken to ensure my safety. I know my mom's family would like to believe that they would have been able to help me. As much as anyone wants to believe this, I cannot. This belief was further reinforced 20 years later when they continued to support Mike even after he was arrested for soliciting a minor and my abuse had been brought to light. After he killed himself I was told "You will not tarnish his memory" and to this day, the family photos still hang on the wall as though nothing has changed.
>
> My paternal grandma was "my person" growing up. It's funny because I always knew we were close, and she meant a lot to me, but it wasn't until she passed in 2013 that I started to see just how important she was to my development. She was a place I always knew I was okay. I was loved and accepted, truly, no matter what. Even when we would argue and fight, which we did, I always knew we would be okay. My brother used to tell me that we fought like best friends. And we were just that, best friends. She knew my friends, all through life. What middle and high school kids actually want to go hang out with their friend's grandma to play and have dinner? Mine did. And I knew her friends, and what was going on in their lives, and knew where they were going for their Saturday morning breakfast club.
>
> I believe as an adult as I learn to cope and process everything, resilience is a choice I make. I choose to be resilient. I am constantly forcing myself to face things I do not want to, and that do not come naturally. It means learning to be open. It means surrendering everything, realizing that I don't know what to do, and being willing to try and to learn new ways. So, when I was a child, my resilience enabled me to "get through" and survive, while now as an adult, it enables me to be open and find new ways of coping and continuing to thrive as I utilize the things I've learned to help others. I believe that no matter how difficult or scary it may be, you cannot expect different results if you keep trying the same things.

Resilience after trauma

How does resilience "work"? Resilience research has experienced what Masten (2007) calls three waves of focus: understanding the trajectories of development revealing "unexpectedly positive adaptation or recovery after adversity" (p. 921); explaining processes that account for the presence of these trajectories (e.g., attachment relationships, family environment); and testing these hypothesized processes through interventions designed to promote resilience in children at risk of adverse outcomes. The fourth wave is psychobiological, considering how adversity exists in the brain or in body systems, and how resilience operates at that level. Thus, a clear understanding of resilience's mechanisms for buffering trauma and increasing well-being is not yet possible. It is clear, however, that certain factors previously identified as protective factors have the effect of building resources and intensifying their use.

Some research suggests that concepts considered in this text also influence the positive process of resilience: hope, positive emotions, and self-compassion. For example, Kong et al. (2018) studied the trauma of diagnosed infertility among a large (over 1000) sample of women. Resilience was most effective in producing post-traumatic growth when the women experienced high levels of positive emotions. Among adolescents (Bluth, Mullarkey, & Lathren, 2018), self-compassion was highly associated with curiosity/exploration (recall the broaden and build model presented in Chapter 4) and with resilience.

Another example of a protective factor is spiritual/religious systems of belief. As will be discussed in Chapter 8, this system provides opportunities for healthy attachment, for meaningfulness, for support, and for religious rituals, all of which have been shown to increase emotional security and self-regulation. Park, Currier, Harris, and Slattery (2017) outline a range of spiritual and related resources associated with greater resilience. These resources pertain to beliefs, goals, meaning, coping, and social connections. For example, within meaning resources are strengths such as hope, optimism, and acceptance. Notice how Kimberly addresses this factor in her life.

> I would be doing a disservice if I did not explain how my faith played an insurmountable role in everything. I did not grow up with church, although most of my friends growing up were Catholic. I thought that praying meant you had to say certain things, and do certain things with your hands, or it "didn't count." As I learned more about church, and religion, and God, I came to understand that I had in fact prayed while growing up. I guess I just thought I was talking to "someone" or "something." I knew there was something bigger than us in life, but I didn't understand. As I mentioned earlier, I started to shape this belief from everything going on with my dad's health. I learned how very little control we actually have in life. With this realization that we lack control, it was clear to me that you had better seek guidance from someone who does.
>
> So, I do see now, looking back, that I actually did have God in my life, and I did pray. I just didn't realize it. I would say that I truly came to know and experience God following the exposure of everything with my stepdad. This is when I actually began to have a relationship with Jesus and started to learn more and understand the Holy Spirit. It was not until looking back

through my journal later though, that I found that as I would be journaling, that I would randomly drop into prayer. I would be writing and then find, "Dear God, please be with me. Please show me the way. I literally do not know what to do. . .give me the strength and the courage."

During this time as an adult, I also came to be grateful that my dad and my grandma had already passed away. During a time when I felt completely, and utterly, alone, they were with me. No doubt in my mind. It was the worst isolation and I would not wish that upon an enemy. It was one of those scenarios where you could be with your best friend, or your spouse, yet feel completely alone. That's what sexual abuse does to you. I actually came to have this vision that got me through the lowest times. I would pray for God to lead, walk ahead of me, and show me the way. Then I would call upon my grandma and my dad to walk on either side of me to carry me as I should stumble. I know they carried me through the worst of it.

Promoting resilience

Interventions developed to increase resilience have been investigated among children and adults. Among children, these interventions target several participant levels: children themselves, their caregivers and/or teachers, and systems in which they function (school, community). For example, Merrell (2010) conducted the Oregon Resiliency Project in which school settings served as the base for interventions whose aim was to enhance skills associated with resilience; examples are social skills and problem-solving skills. Programs that target positive youth development address both protective and risk factors in families, peer groups, schools and communities. A recent meta-analysis (Taylor, Oberle, Durlak, & Weissberg, 2017) found that follow-up data from positive youth development program revealed children's gains in emotional well-being, academic success, and social behavior.

Adult interventions are more likely focused on the psychological functioning of the participants. An example is a study (Miller, Liossis, Shochet, Biggs, & Donald, 2008) that implemented *Promoting Adult Resilience* in a workplace setting. This program was based on cognitive–behavioral methods with a positive psychology context, and included information on identifying personal strengths, managing stress, using effective self-talk, increasing problem-solving skills, and learning skills for managing interpersonal conflict. Outcomes were favorable, with reduced depression and increased confidence in coping among participants, and the outcomes were maintained at a follow-up.

The focus of this text is on clinicians promoting positive strengths among their clients to increase their ability to be present in their lives. These strengths are desirable in their own right and also serve as resilience resources during times of adversity. Using resilience language, these strengths are both assets and protective factors. McAdams (1995) presented a three part model that is an excellent way of communicating with clients regarding resilience. Level 1 are personality traits possessed by individuals ("having"). Level 2 are personal goals and efforts that influence daily responses ("doing"). Level 3 are life stories and narratives that create meaning ("being"). All of these levels are discussed by positive psychologists, but having a model of their operation may be of assistance to clients as they organize their own pictures of resilience.

While it may be appealing to think of resilience as a single strength that can be increased during intervention, that conclusion is not well-supported by research literature or by theoretical and empirical models. Rather, resilience might be thought of as the process of identifying important strengths, and enhancing resilience as the ancillary outcome of a personal journey. These strengths have been and will be discussed in this text; examples are optimism, hope, and meaning.

Iacoviello and Charney (2014) do identify practical behaviors for cultivating resilience during a personal journey. First is finding a resilience role model. So often, as discussed in Chapter 1, traumatized people are isolated in their experiences. Having a person who knows the "journey" and is familiar with the "territory" is a great help. Second is establishing a social network. Support from encouraging others builds positive emotions in the self and motivation for adaptive coping. Third is having physical activity. Van der Kolk (2014) notes the importance of learning to be physically present in one's body after trauma, an experience that reverses the avoidance of sensory stimuli occurring during trauma. Fourth is designating personal strengths, and learning how each strength can be a companion for the journey. Last is learning how to face fear rather than avoid fear. This last behavior is critical for being able to learn from the present rather than being frozen out of new experiences.

Kimberly considered ways to help someone have resilience after trauma.

> To me, resilience can be broken down into attitudes and actions, three of each. The first attitude, I call, "Clean your closet". The best way to explain what I did with everything that had happened to me is I kept it on the shelf in the closet of my mind. The evening of August 31, 2014, my brother called to tell me that my stepdad had been arrested for soliciting a minor. He had placed an ad on Craigslist for a daddy-daughter fantasy. This moment changed my life forever. That box in the closet spilled all over the floor, never to be the same again. My counselor explained to me that the closet was a good analogy for a choice to make. I could step over everything that had spilled all over but the mess would remain. I could scoop it all up back into the box and shove it back in the closet. Yet the mess would again remain. Or I could sort through it all, getting rid of some things, while choosing to reorganize the rest of it.
>
> Attitude two is "Own your feelings." I remember back in my Interpersonal Communications class in high school when our teacher shared the idea that nobody can make you feel anything. People can do things to you, and things can happen, but only you are able to choose how you allow yourself to feel. I remember being so excited to learn this. But when I shared my excitement that night at the dinner table, I was met with opposition. I remember being told this was dumb, and if this was the case then why would anyone willingly choose to feel sad, hurt, or angry. I tried to explain that things will happen and people can do things, but ultimately, it's up to you how you let that affect you. This idea that I viewed as offering power and freedom was rejected by my family.
>
> "Have some bad days" is the third attitude. We are quick to think we should be feeling and doing better than we are. As a society, everyone wants a quick fix. Sometimes when life happens, there is no quick fix. In the event of trauma, it takes time to process through grief, particularly if you're going to do so in a healthy manner. I can recall multiple people thinking I needed to get medication, and they couldn't understand why I wasn't taking something, even

just to "take the edge off." This is an important lesson, to never allow someone else's discomfort with your grief to shame or guilt you into feeling something different. Now, with this comes the responsibility that if you experience several consecutive horrible days in a row, you should seek professional help.

The first action is to "Resist the urge to run." For me, when I had so many emotions stirring inside of me, I would feel as though I needed to literally run. I would feel so wound up and anxious inside, and I truly didn't know what to do with it. I am usually, or used to be, a very laid-back person, so to feel such intense feelings of anxiety was foreign to me. I would have moments where my emotions would erupt as I couldn't hold them inside any longer.

My counselor gave me guidance on how to fight through this urge to run. He first had me commit to not leaving. I had to commit that I simply would not allow myself to leave my husband and kids. But during those moments where I so badly felt that urge to head for the hills, he told me to force myself to sit with it. And when I felt I couldn't possibly hold it in any longer, push myself even just five more minutes. But then, allow myself to leave my boys with my husband and go for a drive and get away. So often I would just go drive, windows down, music loud, either singing or bawling. So each time I would get that urge to run, I would eventually allow myself to escape, however only after forcing myself to sit with the discomfort just a little longer than the previous time.

"Become your own best friend" is the second action. I noticed early on that my friends would regularly come to me for advice, so I figured I must provide decent feedback. I realized that if I could just talk to myself as I would my best friend that I could do alright. When I would find myself wondering what to do, I would step back and ask myself, "what would you tell your own best friend?" I find this particularly helpful when dealing with difficult things in life because when friends share their stories, we are more likely to respond with empathy, kindness and compassion. When we talk to ourselves, we tell ourselves it's not that bad, and to suck it up and handle it, or that we should be "over it" by now.

The third action is probably the most difficult. I call it "Review your roster." One of the greatest struggles for me through everything was my mom's family and how they handled things. At first, they couldn't get past my mom and how things affected her. My feelings didn't matter. They were angry, and maybe still are, that I was not there "for my mom" to help plan Mike's funeral. Yes, in their minds, I should have been there to support my mom as they sorted through family photos and shared stories as they all planned my stepdad's funeral. The man that had molested me.

One day I realized that my family hadn't left me, but I was making the choice not to have them. I tell people that my team may be smaller now, but it is way more powerful and better. I may not have as much family in my life now, but that's okay. It's funny how much family loyalty was preached to me, and how we were always told how "family is everything" and "blood is thicker than water" while growing up. Fortunately as I've become an independent adult I have come to learn that what really matters is not your DNA but rather what is in a person's heart. What matters is the love and respect you mutually share.

From these six attitudes and actions, you can see that resilience isn't something you simply have or do not have. It is something you do, and something you choose. Decisions can be made that help you grow and evolve as a person. None of these things I explained are easy. But it boils down to realizing where you currently are, and if you want things to change, you have to do something. You have to be willing to face things that scare you but do it anyways. It makes me laugh when people sometimes refer to me as "fearless" because I think of all the times I have faced things that absolutely terrify me. The difference is I have learned to do it anyway. I am confident that if you are willing to try new things, willing to stretch yourself and get uncomfortable, that you too can demonstrate "resilience."

Summary

One positive psychology strength that we especially consider during development is resilience. Resilience is identified by its presence: children and adolescents who are at risk, who have experienced one or more adversities that have been shown to influence impairment, instead show positive adaptation. Similarly, among adults, resilience occurs as they respond to traumatic events with fewer problems and more competence. Masten (2001) emphasizes the importance of viewing resilience as *ordinary magic*: as the influence of ordinary processes rather than extraordinary processes in service of the individual having "good outcomes in spite of serious threats to adaptation or development" (p. 228). This view should reassure and inspire clinicians to encourage clients to consider their own normally occurring capacities and abilities as essential forces in life after trauma.

References

Bluth, K., Mullarkey, M., & Lathren, C. (2018). Self-compassion: A potential path to adolescent resilience and positive exploration. *Journal of Child and Family Studies*, *27*, 3037–3047. Available from https://doi.org/10.1007/s10826-018-1125-1.

Bonanno, G. A. (2004). Loss, trauma, and human resilience: Have we underestimated the human capacity to thrive after extremely aversive events? *American Psychologist*, *59*, 20–28.

Campbell-Sills, L., & Stein, M. B. (2007). Psychometric analysis and refinement of the Connor-Davidson Resilience Scale (CD-RISC): Validation of a 10-item measure of resilience. *Journal of Traumatic Stress*, *20*, 1019–1028.

Felitti, V. J., Anda, R. F., Nordenberg, D., Williamson, D. F., Spitz, A. M., Edwards, V., ... Marks, J. S. (1998). Relationship of childhood abuse and household dysfunction to many of the leading causes of death in adults. *American Journal of Preventive Medicine*, *14*, 245–258.

Freud, A., & Burlingham, D. T. (1943). *War and children*. New York, NY: Medical War Books.

Iacoviello, B. M., & Charney, D. S. (2014). Psychosocial facets of resilience: Implications for preventing posttrauma psychopathology, treating trauma survivors, and enhancing community resilience. *European Journal of Psychotraumatology*, *5*, 23970.

Jeste, D. V., Savla, G. N., Thompson, W. K., Vahia, I. V., Glorioso, D. K., Martin, A. S., ... Depp, C. A. (2013). Association between older age and more successful aging: Critical role of resilience and depression. *American Journal of Psychiatry*, *170*, 188–196.

Kong, L., Fang, M., Ma, T., Li, G., Yang, F., Meng, Q., ... Li, P. (2018). Positive affect mediates the relationship between resilience, social support, and posttraumatic growth of women with infertility. *Psychology, Health & Medicine*, *23*, 707–716.

Lopez, S. J., Pedrotti, J. T., & Snyder, C. R. (2015). *Positive psychology: The scientific and practical explorations of human strengths* (3rd ed.). Thousand Oaks, CA: Sage Publications.

Masten, A. S. (2001). Ordinary magic: Resilience processes in development. *American Psychologist*, *56*, 227–238.

Masten, A. S. (2007). Resilience in developing systems: Progress and promise as the fourth wave rises. *Development and Psychopathology*, *19*, 921–930.

Masten, A. S., Cutuli, J. J., Herbers, J. E., & Reed, M. J. (2009). Resilience in development. In S. J. Lopez, & C. R. Snyder (Eds.), *The Oxford handbook of positive psychology* (2nd ed., pp. 117–131). New York, NY: Oxford University Press.

McAdams, D. P. (1995). What do we know when we know a person? *Journal of Personality*, *63*, 365–396.

Merrell, K. W. (2010). Linking prevention science and social and emotional learning: The Oregon Resiliency Project. *Psychology in the Schools*, *47*, 55–70.

Miller, P., Liossis, P., Shochet, I. M., Biggs, H., & Donald, M. (2008). Being on PAR: Outcomes of a pilot trial to improve mental health and wellbeing in the workplace with the Promoting Adult Resilience Program. *Behaviour Change*, *25*, 215–228.

Park, C. L., Currier, J. M., Harris, J. I., & Slattery, J. M. (2017). *Trauma, meaning, and spirituality: Translating research into clinical practice*. Washington, DC: American Psychological Association.

Taylor, R. D., Oberle, E., Durlak, J. A., & Weissberg, R. P. (2017). Promoting positive youth development through school-based social and emotional learning interventions: A meta-analysis of follow-up effects. *Child Development*, *88*, 1156–1171.

Van der Kolk, B. (2014). The body keeps the score: Brain, mind, and body in the healing of trauma. New York, NY: Viking.

Werner, E. E. (1993). Risk, resilience, and recovery: Perspectives from the Kauai Longitudinal Study. *Development and Psychopathology*, *5*, 503–515.

Werner, E. E., & Smith, R. S. (1982). *Vulnerable but invincible: A study of resilient children*. New York, NY: McGraw-Hill.

Werner, E. E., & Smith, R. S. (1992). *Overcoming the odds: High risk children from birth to adulthood*. Ithaca, NY: Cornell University Press.

Resources for clinicians and clients

Goldstein, S., & Brooks, R. B. (2013). *Handbook of resilience in children* (2nd ed.). New York, NY: Springer.

Moss, W. L. (2016). *Bounce back: How to be a resilient kid*. Washington, DC: American Psychological Association.

Neimark, J. (2016). *The hugging tree: A story about resilience*. Washington, DC: American Psychological Association.

Reich, J. W., Zautra, A. J., & Hall, J. S. (Eds.), (2012). *Handbook of adult resilience*. New York, NY: Guildford Press.

Sandberg, S., & Grant, A. (2017). *Option B: facing adversity, building resilience, and finding joy*. New York, NY: Alfred A. Knopf.

Forgiveness

6

Positive psychology suggests that an individual's well-being occurs within, and is influenced by, his or her relationships with others. For example, Seligman's (2017) PERMA model includes relationships as one aspect of pleasure and engagement. Specific strengths and virtues, such as temperance, humanity, and justice, are only realized in living among others (see Peterson & Seligman, 2004). Lopez, Pedrotti, and Snyder (2015) noted that two foundations exist beneath the strengths that operate within relationships. The first foundation is empathy, an orientation toward perceiving and understanding others that manifests itself in strengths of altruism, gratitude, and forgiveness. The second is attachment, an orientation toward loving others that results in relationship bonds.

Interpersonal ties and the foundations of empathy and attachment are damaged by trauma in many ways. At the inception, the nature of trauma creates a break in normal bonds with others. For example, trauma creates a sense of aloneness, and of a failure to be understood. As another example, trauma may be intentionally or unintentionally caused by another person or persons. These traumas may be physical, emotional, social, or cultural in nature, or a combination of the above, and their infliction on the victim by another person exacerbates their impact. In fact, even when traumas are created by natural forces, their destruction is often experienced as a personal attack. It is worth returning to how trauma was described by Herman (1992):

> *Psychological trauma is an affliction of the powerless. At the moment of trauma, the victim is rendered helpless by overwhelming force. When the force is that of nature, we speak of disasters. When that force is that of other human beings, we speak of atrocities. Traumatic events overwhelm the ordinary systems of care that give people a sense of control, connection, and meaning. (p. 33).*

Traumas intentionally caused by actions of others are experienced by victims as deeply wounding. For example, Schultz, Tallman, and Altmaier (2010) studied 146 community-living adults who responded to a research solicitation for persons who had been "significantly wronged" by another person or persons. As part of the study, participants wrote an open-ended transgression narrative later categorized by raters. The categories revealed a wide range of interpersonal transgressions, including sexual assault, physical harm, infidelity, slander, and betrayal. Participants rated the impact of these interpersonal transgressions on a measure of event-related distress. These ratings revealed that even traumas as benign-sounding as "slander" caused distress comparable to that experienced by persons diagnosed with posttraumatic stress disorder (PTSD).

Promoting Positive Processes after Trauma. DOI: https://doi.org/10.1016/B978-0-12-811975-4.00006-X
Copyright © 2019 Elsevier Inc. and Kimberly Gleason. All rights reserved.

However, traumas do not have to be intentionally caused by the actions of others in order to create a sense of being personally wounded. For example, Roxberg, Burman, Guldbrand, Fridlund, and da Silva (2010) interviewed survivors of the 2004 tsunami created by an earthquake beneath the Indian Ocean, one of the deadliest natural disasters ever recorded that resulted in deaths and devastation in 14 countries. These interviews documented that a common response after disaster was to place blame on someone or some agency outside of oneself, leading to anger, resentment, and bitterness. This conclusion was also noted by Worthington et al. (2016) as they drew a parallel between post-trauma resentment, bitterness and depression, and the experience of unforgiveness. Examples of external blamed targets are persons who should have triggered an earlier warning, first responders, non-responsive community and federal government employees, and even other victims who experienced the disaster.

This chapter considers the strength of forgiveness as one means by which traumas, particularly those committed by another, can be mitigated. In this chapter, theory and research regarding forgiveness, including forgiveness of others and self-forgiveness, as well as variables that influence forgiveness is presented. How forgiveness buffers the effects of trauma is a primary interest, as well as how clinicians can promote forgiveness. In this chapter, too, are Kimberly's responses to the following definition and questions:

Forgiveness definition

A response by an individual, or a group of individuals, to being hurt, offended, or harmed by another person or group of individuals. Forgiveness is a process involving thoughts, feelings, and behaviors where anger, revenge, bitterness, and avoidance are replaced with empathy, good will, and benevolence toward the offender.

Forgiveness is not condoning or excusing the offense, or justifying the offender; forgiveness is also not reconciliation, a process that requires the active participation of both victim and offender.

Forgiveness questions

Forgiveness begins with the acknowledgment that an actual offense was committed, and with the refusal to somehow excuse or justify that offense. Do you remember having this happen in your past?

Were there influences in your life away from forgiveness? Toward forgiveness? What examples of either or both do you remember?

Do you see short- or long-term effects of unforgiveness in your life? Do you see effects of forgiveness?

Forgiveness has been linked to growth after trauma. Have you experienced this juxtaposition in your life, where forgiveness allowed you to have one or more of the following: new directions, appreciation of life, spiritual change, improved relationships with others, personal strengths?

What might help someone else increase their own experience of forgiveness?

Defining forgiveness

Similar to other virtues and strengths discussed in this book, forgiveness is an ancient ideal. All of the world's major religions present teachings on forgiveness. Many philosophers over time have also written on forgiveness, for example, analyzing who has standing to forgive a transgression (see Pettigrove (2009) for a discussion of second- and third-party forgiveness). However, it is only within the past 30 or so years that the scholarly study of forgiveness as a psychological construct has rapidly increased.

Defining forgiveness is a complicated task. Several variations of a psychological definition of forgiveness have focused on different components of the forgiveness response. The victim's motivations toward the offender are the center of McCullough's model (see McCullough, 2008; McCullough & Witvliet, 2000). Forgiveness in motivational terms entails the victim giving up negative motivations, such as revenge and avoidance, and adopting positive motivations (e.g., benevolence) toward the offender. Emotional forgiveness, replacing negative emotions about the offender with prosocial emotions such as sympathy or compassion, is the focus of Worthington's model (see Wade & Worthington, 2003). Worthington (2005) also described decisional forgiveness, an explicit decision by the victim to change one's behaviors toward the offender away from negative actions (e.g., aggression). Last, Enright and Fitzgibbons (2000) describe forgiveness as a process, rather than a single event, in which the victim gradually replaces negative thoughts, feelings, and behaviors toward or about the offender with more positive thoughts, feelings, and behaviors.

In spite of varying emphases in definitions of forgiveness, there is agreement over what concepts are not the same as forgiveness. Forgiveness, for example, is not condoning the offense. *Condoning*, which is exemplified by the statement, "It wasn't that big a deal," minimizes the severity of the impact of the offense or trauma on the victim and redefines an interpersonal offense as acceptable. Forgiveness is also not justifying, when the purported reasons behind the offense supposedly balance its impact (e.g., "he was just having a bad day," "She didn't really mean it"). Avoiding a confrontation because of anxiety, being unwilling to acknowledge one's own anger over an offense, and "forgetting" the event are also responses that are not forgiveness. *Reconciliation* is also not forgiveness; reconciliation is a two-person process where both people (transgressor, victim) work toward restoring a relationship to its prior status before the offense. Forgiveness can happen without reconciliation.

A model proposed by Fehr, Gelfand, and Nag (2010) identified variables that influence the occurrence of forgiveness. Cognitive influences on forgiveness pertain to the victim's attitudes and thoughts concerning the offender and the event. These influences include the responsibility the victim attributes to the offender, the severity of the harm perceived by the victim, and the degree of rumination engaged in by the victim. Emotional influences include both positive and negative mood, empathy (feelings of warmth and compassion toward another), and anger. In their analysis, Fehr et al. provided evidence that when victims perceive the offense as severe and intentionally caused, and when victims ruminate over the offense, they report less forgiveness. In terms of emotional influences, when victims have negative mood and anger, they are less likely to forgive, but when they have empathy for the offender, they are more likely to forgive.

Kimberly found that forgiveness influenced her recovery, although in varying ways that reflect the nature of the relationships in which she exercised forgiveness.

> After much deliberation, I realized that I must do whatever I had to do to help the police uncover Mike's mess and to understand what exactly had taken place, no matter the consequences. Ultimately, I did help the police with the case against my stepfather. And although I knew it is not my fault, he did end up killing himself from the pressure of his world of deceit and lies closing in around him. For me to be able to sleep at night, and look at myself in the mirror come morning, I had to risk losing it all. I knew what I had to do following Mike's arrest, but I also had to hold onto the hope that one day my mom would be able to understand my position and forgive me as well.
>
> And for all intents and purposes, I did lose my mom. The mom I grew up with was no longer. You simply cannot go through such trauma and come out unchanged. Even if you choose to deny it all, it will unknowingly change you. Following Mike's death, my mom and I slowly began to talk through things and rebuild a relationship. With time and space, and many conversations with law enforcement and my counselor, I came to better understand my mom's position and gained insight and further empathy for her.
>
> The first time someone asked me if I would ever be able to forgive my mom for not believing me, and for standing by my stepdad as things played out from his arrest through his death, I was surprised. Even though I had an incredible anger and immense hurt from the pain and loneliness which I felt, I never really had to intentionally work at forgiving my mom. I so badly wanted and needed my mom back in my life, and this is where the journey of forgiveness began without my even knowing it. My dad and my paternal grandmother, who was my best friend, had already died. Now my stepfather had killed himself, which tore my mom's family apart. So having my mom back and willing to work through things was all the motivation I needed to forgive. All the anger, and believe me there was plenty, faded over time. The relationship my mom and I share today is drastically different than the one we had before. And though there is a loss of the relationship that was, I hold onto knowing that different does not mean less. In many ways our relationship today is much more free and authentic because it is a relationship we've rebuilt, not the one assigned at birth.
>
> With Mike, my stepdad, I knew right away I would have to find a way to forgive him. I knew it might be a long time before that would come, but nonetheless, it would be necessary. Forgiveness was going to be how I released his grip on me, bring that freedom I so badly wanted, and regain my power. I was tired of him having power and control over me. It would be through forgiveness that I would be able to loosen his grip on me, and be free. I knew this would be how I could "win" and overcome what he had done to me and take back what he stole from me.
>
> Once I felt as though I had forgiven Mike, or at least traveled a distance on that journey, I physically felt different. I felt lighter; I felt free. I felt as though I could breathe again, that I was free to be me, and that I had more control of my life and my emotions. It no longer made me want to vomit if my boys made a comment about missing their grandpa. I found it easier to talk to my mom about her feelings as well, because I didn't have underlying feelings of my

> own. I guess the biggest thing was the abuse and the trauma from the exposure of it changed from being something that had this strong hold on me, and weighed me down, to something that happened and certainly does not define me. And maybe that's why I am more able to now look at my "story" as just that. I know that I did not choose to have this story. And I did not choose to have things exposed as they were. But, I do get to control what to do with it now.

Forgiveness after trauma

If victims forgive their offenders, does that response affect their own mental health? There are many studies that document the positive association of forgiveness with better psychological well-being. An initial review by Worthington and Scherer (2004) established that forgiveness improved emotional health (reduced depression, increased happiness) and intensified life satisfaction. That finding of improved mental health associated with forgiveness was reiterated by a review conducted by Hill, Heffernan, and Allemand (2015). More recently, Akhtar and Barlow (2018) performed a meta-analysis of studies in which participants received forgiveness-promoting interventions. Data revealed that increases in forgiveness due to these programs promoted positive emotionality and improved mental health among the participants.

Forgiveness also has been associated with physical health and with certain physiological mechanisms that influence health. For example, Witvliet, Ludwig, and Vander Laan (2001) used a laboratory setting to compare the action of forgiveness to the action of holding a grudge: unforgiveness, holding a grudge, created higher stress responses (e.g., EMG, heart rate, blood pressure) than forgiveness. More recently, Seawall, Toussaint, and Cheadle (2014) examined the longitudinal relationship of forgiveness with physical health among a large (over 1000) sample of adults. Lack of forgiveness at the initial time of assessment was associated with physical health decline between the first assessment and the follow-up.

Is self-forgiveness a relevant concept to this discussion? Self-forgiveness is similar to forgiving others, in that the action involves a willingness to reduce negative feelings, thoughts, and actions toward the self after an objective wrong. This action is more than "letting oneself off the hook:" rather, it is a process of recognizing wrong was committed, experiencing guilt, doing self-analysis, and granting forgiveness to the self. There is less research on self-forgiveness, and that research has provided evidence both for and against positive effects. A recent study by Peterson et al. (2017) studied self-forgiveness among adults and revealed that self-forgiving feelings and beliefs were associated with reduced self-harm (i.e., disordered eating) and reduced self-rejection among perpetrators.

More recently, Cornish, Woodyatt, Morris, Conroy, and Townsdin (2018) directly compared self-forgiveness to self-exoneration ("letting oneself off the hook"). In a series of studies, participants identified specific offenses they had committed against others that still created personal distress and completed measures of responsibility, self-punishment and self-forgiveness, and empathic concern. Data revealed three clusters of association linked with three separate actions. The first was self-condemning; these persons accepted responsibility but continued to self-condemn and did not self-forgive. The second cluster was self-exonerating; these persons did not accept responsibility for the transgression and were less self-condemning but were not self-forgiving. The last cluster was self-forgiveness, with high levels of personal responsibility, high self-forgiveness, and low self-condemnation.

How does the action of forgiveness create positive responses associated with it? The most straightforward explanation is that forgiveness improves mental and physical health because it reduces inappropriate or harmful responses, such as seeking revenge, and increases beneficial responses, such as those that foster emotional regulation. Witvliet and Luna (2018) note that these beneficial responses include processing information that increases compassion for the offender, experiencing positive emotions about the offender, and seeking social support and relational closeness.

Another explanation is that forgiveness interrupts a cycle that can lead to *chronic embitterment*. A special section in the journal, *Psychological Trauma: Theory, Research, Practice, and Policy* ("Posttraumatic embitterment syndrome", 2018) considered the phenomenon of three interrelated processes after a trauma. The first process is that the person is angry and bitter, and views these responses as appropriate given the injustice of the traumatic event. The second process is that the person "holds on" to beliefs that he or she has a right to this anger and an equal right to demand restitution from an offender. The third process is that this ongoing rumination fortifies repeated and intrusive recall of the event.

These reactions are similar in some ways to PTSD. One similarity is that the event is perceived to violate the core belief of a just world. The second similarity is that the event triggers rumination. A third similarity is that chronic embitterment and PTSD both build multiple types of impairment in social roles such as work or family. The difference between embitterment and PTSD is that the affective state of embitterment is anger, or rage, and helplessness rather than the deep fear and anxiety that characterizes PTSD.

A third explanation of how forgiveness creates benefits is that the victim of the offense uses the experience as an opportunity. Finding benefit is a positive reappraisal process that identifies benefits in the midst of adversity. These benefits might be personal, such as an increase of empathy for others in similar circumstances, or increase in personal strengths such as insight. Benefits can also be noted in improved relationships, in the discovering of new life directions, and in increased spirituality. Using forgiveness in response to an interpersonal trauma may reflect the victim's realization that the trauma has created a potential for benefits that influence on his or her future life.

Kimberly considered how forgiveness worked in her life to reverse its ugliness and to heal its wounds.

> I firmly believe that ignoring the abuse and the wounds it inflicted continues to harm us. We are not even aware of the effects. They may come in the form of how we cannot fully connect with others on an intimate level. We constantly feel as though we are waiting for the bottom to fall out of our world. We avoid certain behaviors with others, something as simple as whispering, because it triggers things. Effects may also show up in the form of unexplained angry outbursts. Before we can hope to forgive, we must first acknowledge the existence of a wound.

Burying your head in the sand not only influences us, but also our loved ones and society as a whole away from forgiveness.

Often, we forget that we need to forgive ourselves. As victims, we blame ourselves and think we should have seen it coming, or that we somehow made them think we wanted it. We blame ourselves over and over again. So often we think of forgiving others, but what about forgiving ourselves? This was a huge step for me, particularly how things played out with my dad. You see, Mike literally destroyed the relationship I had with my dad. He would constantly say that if my dad loved me, he would do ABC, and if he loved me, he wouldn't do XYZ. One of the biggest problems I had with my abuse was the damage it did to my relationship with my dad, and he died when I was 19. There was no going back; I could not recover that lost time and apologize to my dad for believing Mike's lies. My counselor helped me to see that I was a child, and I could not be held responsible for this, and that my dad would not want me to blame myself.

After making huge strides in forgiving Mike, I was able to more easily tell my story, and have the confidence to think larger scale in using my story to help others. It was this freedom and peace I had found that helped me accept that I now have a "story". This was hard for me to grasp initially as I see myself as an ordinary person, nothing special, just an everyday mom and wife. But as I progressed on this journey, and worked through forgiving, it became easier to accept that I have this story, like it or not. My goal now is to figure out how I can utilize what I've learned through my own counseling, endless introspection, and many conversations with various professionals who work with survivors of sexual abuse to help other survivors progress on their healing journeys as well as educate others how to better respond when sexual abuse is brought to light.

I get asked if I feel responsible for Mike's death, and the answer is no. I know that it is not my fault. He made the choices that got him in the mess, and also made the choice of how to end it. This was Mike's work of evil. I've also been asked if I'm happy he's dead. The answer is no, I'm not happy. However, since Mike did what he did, and made the choice to end things, I have come to find relief in that. As I was struggling with PTSD following the exposure and his death, I would "see" his face when I would close my eyes, or "see" him standing behind me or over my shoulder, I had the benefit to assure myself that he was dead.

PTSD is awful because you literally feel as though you're going crazy and losing your mind. I had seen Mike in his casket so I could assure myself that he was dead and that my mind was playing tricks on me. I also did not have to deal with going to trial, testifying against both him and my mom's family as they supported him. I don't have to worry about when he's going to get out of prison, and possibly running into him again. My boys can know he's dead and that's why they don't get to see him anymore. No further explanation is needed at their young ages. So again, people ask how I feel about his death. I'm not "happy" he's dead. I have, however, come to see that there are benefits for me and my family to know he is no longer a threat to us or any other children.

Promoting forgiveness

Recall that traumas create an inclination toward avoidance: avoidance of others, avoidance of stimuli associated with the trauma, and avoidance of a perpetrator. Avoidance is negatively reinforced by relief from those unwanted experiences, thereby decreasing any opportunity for learning or change. Because avoidance plays a significant role in depression beyond the role of anxiety and rumination (Moulds, Kandris, Starr, & Wong, 2007), decreasing avoidance is essential in reducing depression and increasing well-being. A study of 120 low-income adults with trauma histories (Green, 2011) considered forgiveness and avoidance as pathways to posttraumatic growth. In this study, both increased forgiveness and decreased avoidance were routes of increasing growth and reducing distress. Avoidance was negatively and directly related to forgiveness, suggesting forgiveness was a means of dealing with avoidance.

Forgiveness may reduce avoidance through empathy. While empathy was traditionally defined as "the ability to feel and describe the thoughts and feelings of others" (Dymond, 1948), later researchers created multidimensional conceptualizations of empathy. Davis (1983) considered empathy as the "reactions of one individual to the observed experiences of another" (p. 113). In teasing apart those reactions, Davis identified three specific components. The first was perspective taking: being able and willing to subsume the self in service to understanding the reactions of others. The second is empathic concern: feeling sympathy and concern for others. The last is personal distress: being able to manage one's own anxiety in the presence of high levels of distress in others.

Forgiveness may also reduce avoidance through strengths of altruism and gratitude. Altruistic behaviors occur for the benefit of another person. Apparently altruistic behaviors (see Lopez et al., 2015) can be motived by selfish reasons, however, as when such a behavior is seen to increase the likelihood of personal gain. Or altruism can occur for egotistic reasons, such as to see oneself in a favorable light. Forgiveness has been referred to as an altruistic gift to the perpetrator (see Oliner, 2005).

Gratitude pertains to feelings and reactions of appreciation, sometimes in response to the behavior of another, sometimes in response to a natural event such as a beautiful sunset or a spectacular vista. It is a current fashion to focus on gratitude; a search of an online retailer for gratitude-increasing diaries, calendars, and planners revealed over 5000 options! Why is gratitude so emphasized? One reason is that increasing gratitude appears to increase positive emotions; Nezlek, Krejtz, Rusanowska, and Holas (2018) followed over 100 community-living adults on a daily basis for two weeks. Gratitude was related to well-being on a within-person basis. Further, on days where daily events were more negative, this relationship of gratitude to well-being was stronger.

Notice Kimberly's empathy and perspective taking in her relationships with her mother and her stepfather.

> I used to believe it was easier for me to forgive my stepdad because he was dead. I knew what I was dealing with, and there was not much evolving as he was no longer here. But just as I thought I had forgiven him, in the fall of 2016 I discovered his web of deceit far exceeded anything I could imagine. I had saved my report and visual aids from when Mike came to my high school class to speak about what it was like to be a Vietnam veteran. The problem is that now I have his military file, and when I read it I learned he was actually stationed in Hawaii during the war. He did not see combat or personally experience the horrific events he used to tell us about such as what it was like to kill people and watching his buddies blow up in landmines just steps ahead of him. As if it was not enough that he lied about this, it got worse. He claimed that when he was in the war he received a disabling head injury. This head injury caused him to have seizures, which meant he could not work. And because he could not work,

he stayed home and took care of my brother and me since I was five years old. Such a creative way to gain access for his sexual deviances. When this massive deceit was uncovered, I found myself needing to forgive yet another layer. And though it was easier the second time because I knew he was not worth the burden and damage that unforgiveness would cause me, it was nonetheless another layer. I experienced firsthand that forgiveness is not a one-time incident but rather it occurs and unfolds in layers.

I believe that forgiveness is a step of faith. You know your circumstance is beyond your control and you are letting go, severing the hold the offense has on you. And you free yourself of the bitterness, and anger, and animosity, allowing yourself space you need to feel the pain, and grieve and process through it. This may sound like an odd tradeoff to open yourself up to pain and grief. You have to allow yourself to feel the pain before you can hope to go forward in freedom. To truly free yourself you must allow yourself to fully feel it, experience it, process it, and then choose to move forward.

Some of the most honest and pure advice I have ever received on the topic of forgiveness was from my youngest son at age five. I was getting ready to speak on the topic of forgiveness and out of my own interest I asked him if he knew what it meant to forgive someone. He responded instantly, looking slightly annoyed at why I would ask him such a question. After rolling his eyes and huffing, he said, "Mo-om, it means you give it to God." Sometimes we adults like to complicate things, while it's children that keep things simple. After thinking more about this, I realized my son was right. And not only that but I have come to believe myself that trying to forgive without acknowledging God, is like trying to speak a foreign language without first acknowledging the language exist. To me, forgiveness is a concept that is a gift to us from God, and you cannot fully understand its meaning without first acknowledging His existence.

Summary

The focus of this chapter on forgiveness is that it is a strength that occurs in relationships with others, with deeply beneficial effects on the person doing the forgiveness. Whether traumas are caused by others (acts of omission or commission), or whether traumas, external in nature such as a disaster, still promote a "blaming another" response, forgiveness is a positive process for that trauma. The operation of both empathy and attachment assists in healing trauma. Empathy allows us to perceive and understand feelings and actions of others in ways that increase our own gratitude, altruism, and forgiveness. Attachment are loving bonds with others, a propensity to bond or relate to another, that forms the context in which we both receive support from and provide support to other people.

References

Akhtar, S., & Barlow, J. (2018). Forgiveness therapy for the promotion of mental well-being: A systematic review and meta-analysis. *Trauma, Violence, and Abuse*, *19*, 107–122.

Cornish, M. A., Woodyatt, L., Morris, G., Conroy, A., & Townsdin, J. (2018). Self-forgiveness, self-exoneration, and self-condemnation: Individual differences associated with three patterns of responding to interpersonal offenses. *Personality and Individual Differences*, *129*, 43–53.

Davis, M. H. (1983). Measuring individual differences in empathy: Evidence for a multidimensional approach. *Journal of Personality and Social Psychology*, *44*, 113–126.

Dymond, R. (1948). A preliminary investigation of the relation of insight and empathy. *Journal of Consulting Psychology*, *12*, 228–233.

Enright, R. D., & Fitzgibbons, R. P. (2000). *Helping clients forgive: An empirical guide for resolving anger and restoring hope*. Washington, DC: American Psychological Association.

Fehr, R., Gelfand, M. J., & Nag, M. (2010). The road to forgiveness: A meta-analytic synthesis of its situational and dispositional correlates. *Psychological Bulletin*, *136*, 894–914.

Green, M. J. (2011). The role of forgiveness and experiential avoidance in the relationship between posttraumatic growth and distress. *Dissertation Abstracts International*, *72*(3B), 1794.

Herman, J. (1992). *Trauma and recovery*. New York, NY: Basic Books.

Hill, P. L., Heffernan, M. E., & Allemand, M. (2015). Forgiveness and subjective well-being: Discussing mechanisms, contexts, and rationales. In L. L. Toussaint, E. L. Worthington, & D. R. Williams (Eds.), *Forgiveness and health: Scientific evidence and theories relating forgiveness to better health* (pp. 155–169). New York, NY: Springer.

Lopez, S. J., Pedrotti, J. T., & Snyder, C. R. (2015). *Positive psychology: The scientific and practical explorations of human strengths* (3rd ed.). Thousand Oaks, CA: Sage Publications.

McCullough, M. E. (2008). *Beyond revenge: The evolution of the forgiveness instinct*. San Francisco, CA: Jossey-Bass.

McCullough, M. E., & Witvliet, C. V. (2000). The psychology of forgiveness. In C. R. Snyder, & S. J. Lopez (Eds.), *Handbook of positive psychology* (pp. 446–458). New York, NY: Oxford University Press.

Moulds, M. L., Kandris, E., Starr, S., & Wong, A. C. M. (2007). The relationship between rumination, avoidance and depression in a non-clinical sample. *Behaviour Research and Therapy*, *45*, 251–261.

Nezlek, J. B., Krejtz, I., Rusanowska, M., & Holas, P. (2018). Within-person relationships among daily gratitude, well-being, stress, and positive experience. *Journal of Happiness Studies*. Available from https://doi.org/10.1007/s10902-018-9979-x.

Oliner, S. P. (2005). Altruism, forgiveness, empathy, and intergroup apology. *Humboldt Journal of Social Relations*, *29*(2), 8–39.

Peterson, C., & Seligman, M. E. P. (2004). *Character strengths and virtues: A handbook and classification*. Washington, DC: American Psychological Association and New York, NY: Oxford University Press.

Peterson, S. J., Van Tongeren, D. R., Womack, S. D., Hook, J. N., Davis, D. E., & Griffin, B. J. (2017). The benefits of self-forgiveness on mental health: Evidence from correlational and experimental research. *The Journal of Positive Psychology*, *12*, 159–168.

Pettigrove, G. (2009). The standing to forgive. *The Monist*, *92*, 583–603.

Posttraumatic embitterment syndrome. (2018). [Special section]. *Psychological Trauma: Theory, Research, Practice, and Policy*, *10*, 1–57.

Roxberg, A., Burman, M., Guldbrand, M., Fridlund, B., & da Silva, A. B. (2010). Out of the wave: The meaning of suffering and relieved suffering for survivors of the tsunami catastrophe. *Scandinavian Journal of Caring Sciences*, *24*, 707–715.

Schultz, J. M., Tallman, B. A., & Altmaier, E. M. (2010). Pathways to posttraumatic growth: The contribution of forgiveness and importance of religion and spirituality. *Psychology of Religion and Spirituality*, *2*, 104–114.

Seawall, A. H., Toussaint, L. L., & Cheadle, A. C. D. (2014). Prospective association between unforgiveness and physical health and positive mediating mechanisms in a nationally representative sample of older adults. *Psychology and Health, 29*, 374–389.
Seligman, M.E.P. (February 24, 2017). *The PERMA model: Your scientific theory of happiness*. Downloaded from https://positivepsychologyprogram.com/perma-model.
Wade, N. G., & Worthington, E. L. (2003). Overcoming interpersonal offenses: Is forgiveness the only way to deal with unforgiveness? *Journal of Counseling and Development, 81*, 343–353.
Witvliet, C. V. O., Ludwig, T. E., & Vander Laan, K. L. (2001). Granting forgiveness or harboring grudges: Implications for emotion, physiology, and health. *Psychological Science, 12*, 117–123.
Witvliet, C. V. O., & Luna, L. R. (2018). Forgiveness and well-being. In D. S. Dunn (Ed.), *Positive psychology: Established and emerging issues*. New York, NY: Routledge.
Worthington, E. L. (2005). More questions about forgiveness: Research agenda for 2005–2015. In E. L. Worthington (Ed.), *Handbook of forgiveness* (pp. 557–574). New York, NY: Brunner-Routledge.
Worthington, E. L., Griffin, B. J., Toussaint, L. L., Nonterah, C. W., Utsey, S. O., & Garthe, R. C. (2016). Forgiveness as a catalyst for psychological, physical, and spiritual resilience in disasters and crises. *Journal of Psychology and Theology, 44*, 152–165.
Worthington, E. L., & Scherer, M. (2004). Forgiveness is an emotion-focused coping strategy that can reduce health risks and promote health resilience: Theory, review, and hypotheses. *Psychology & Health, 19*, 385–405.

Resources for clinicians and clients

Cantacuzino, M., & Tutu, D. (2015). *The forgiveness project: Stories for a vengeful age*. London, UK: Jessica Kingsley Publishers.
Emmons, R. A. (2016). *The little book of gratitude: Create a life of happiness and wellbeing by giving thanks*. London, UK: Gaia Books. Distributed by Hachette Book Group, New York, NY.
Enright, R. D., & Fitzgibbons, R. P. (2015). *Forgiveness therapy: An empirical guide for resolving anger and restoring hope*. Washington, DC: American Psychological Association.
Mike, D. (2016). *Dishonor: One soldier's journey from desertion to redemption*. Omaha, NE: Dilemma Mike Publishing.
Ten Boom, C. (1971). *The hiding place*. New York, NY: Bantam Book.
The Forgiveness Project. https://www.theforgivenessproject.com.
Tutu, D. (2000). *No future without forgiveness*. New York, NY: Image Book by Doubleday.

Meaning in life

7

How do we discover and/or create meaning in life? While this question might seem the more proper province of philosophers, psychologists are also interested in the function of meaning in life and, relevant to this chapter, meaning in life after trauma. Frankl (1963) is credited with being among those who first highlighted the relationship of trauma to meaning as he wrote about the brutality he experienced while imprisoned in concentration camps during World War II. His observation was that once everything is taken away, including physical and mental necessities, what is left is the choice of attitude in the face of circumstances, the only "human freedom" that cannot be taken away. He entitled his book *Man's Search for Meaning*, denoting motivation to have meaning in general and to create meaning when there appears to be none.

Positive psychology scholars have considered meaning from two contrasting perspectives. The first perspective is that searching for meaning is a "primary motivational force," where every person has an evolving view of the self and its interactions with the external environment. Thus, all of us search for meaning in an ongoing way, even during normal circumstances. The second perspective is that a different type of search for meaning is stimulated when circumstances challenge everyday frameworks of meaning. These two perspectives are not mutually contradictory. In fact, as noted by Steger, Kashdan, Sullivan, and Lorentz (2008), a third option is that searching for meaning occurs under both normal and challenging life circumstances, although whether those searches are the same or different and how they are affected by normal or challenging circumstances is not clear.

Trauma, by definition, disrupts meaning. As noted by Lindy (2006), trauma "confronts the survivor, the therapist, and society at large with contradictions and paradoxes that challenge the assumptions of well-meaning people in a relatively benign universe... Survivors are confronted with a terrifying reality: the ordering principles of the universe, as they had known it, are gone" (p. 321). The trauma literally would not have happened under previously known meanings, and so its occurrence signals that the unknown has taken over. New meanings, therefore, found or reconstructed, will be at the "intersection" of what was known before and what is now unknown.

In this chapter, theory and research concerning the positive process of meaning in life is reviewed. A model of how meaning-making operates after trauma is described. Whether meaning is found or made is considered, as well as more complex questions such as whether all efforts at meaning-making are equally effective. In this chapter, too, are Kimberly's responses to the following definition and questions.

Promoting Positive Processes after Trauma. DOI: https://doi.org/10.1016/B978-0-12-811975-4.00007-1
Copyright © 2019 Elsevier Inc. and Kimberly Gleason. All rights reserved.

Meaning definition

Achieving connection among memory, events, and self-referent beliefs such that the "why" of events is answered; meaning also includes re-appraising the event, grieving loss, and accepting change.
Meaning is making sense of events that otherwise do not make sense, often by finding a benefit for their existence, since those events violate basic assumptions about the world and about the self.
Within the process of coping with challenging events, meaning-making allows events to be accommodated into a system of beliefs and values either by changing those beliefs and values or by changing the perception of the events.

Meaning questions

When did the thought of a "meaning" begin to enter your cognitive and emotional processing of your traumatic experiences? Did you experience a strong felt need to create or find meaning?
Have you been able to create an understanding of why events happened and what benefits you have experienced from them?
Looking back, were there steps you can identify in your process of creating meaning? What were they?
Do you see influences on the meanings that you now have about events that were traumatic?
What do you think might help someone else succeed in the process of making sense and finding benefit from events that appear to not make sense and not have benefit?

Defining meaning

What is the meaning of meaning? Perhaps that sentence is a supreme example of circular definition, where the definition of a term relies on the use of the term itself. The term *meaning* in the English language can connote the sense of a word (e.g., the "meaning" of homeostasis), or a purpose (e.g., what was the "meaning" of that poem), or even a temporal relationship (e.g., that experience was "meaningful"). It should be noted that the term *meaning* has different meanings in different languages. As observed by Baumeister and Landau (2018), meaning is also defined within networks of concepts. So, an event may have one meaning in itself, but another meaning in its connection to or association with another concept. For example, a holiday may confer a particular meaning on an event that would otherwise not have that meaning.

The emphasis of this chapter is on meaning in life. Baumeister and Landau (2018) observed that *meaning in life* encompasses four characteristics. The first is purpose. Meaning in life occurs when events are experienced as related to goals, or to future events, or to hoped-for consequences; those events then have meaning.

The second is mattering. Meaning connotes value; if I mean something to others, then my presence in their lives confers value. I matter to someone. The third is continuity. Meaning occurs as events are connected across time; meanings develop over time and are maintained or changed over time. The fourth is coherence. Coherence occurs as meaning associations fit across a broad spectrum of singular but related events.

From previous chapters, it is obvious that characteristics of purpose, mattering, continuity, and coherence apply to a variety of constructs articulated by positive psychology scholars and clinicians. To explain how meaning in life differs from these other constructs, such as positive emotionality or hope, Steger (2009) proposed a more precise definition of meaning in life: "the extent to which people comprehend, make sense of, or see significance in their lives, accompanied by the degree to which they perceive themselves to have a purpose, mission, or overarching aim in life" (p. 682). Research conducted to validate the recently developed Multidimensional Existential Meaning Scale (George & Park, 2017) demonstrated that separate components of meaning (i.e., comprehension, purpose, and mattering) can be empirically differentiated.

Is meaning in life influential on well-being? Positive psychology certainly theorizes that it is highly influential. Recall that eudaimonic models of well-being are predicated on the importance of meaning to happiness. For example, Ryff (1989) defined six aspects of happiness, of which purpose in life is most related to meaning. Meaning in life is also contained in several virtues (e.g., wisdom, transcendence) and strengths (e.g., perspective, integrity, and spirituality) defined by positive psychology. More recently, Seligman (2017) included meaning as one aspect of happiness defined by his model, PERMA. Therefore, in positive psychology, personal meaning is considered to be intimately related to happiness and well-being in life.

A recent review by Hooker, Masters, and Park (2018) noted that having a greater sense of meaning in life is associated with psychological benefits, and having a lower sense of meaning in life is associated with reduced psychological function. For example, Ho, Cheung, and Cheung (2010) studied over 1800 adolescents regarding the relationship of meaning in life to negative well-being (psychosocial problems) and positive well-being (life satisfaction). Both relationships were supported in their data: meaning was positively associated with well-being and negatively associated with psychosocial problems.

Having greater meaning in life has also been connected with a variety of physical health indicators. Roepke, Jayawickreme, and Riffle (2014) reviewed empirical findings that demonstrated the correlation of a sense of purpose and/or coherence with several general indicators of physical health, including reduced overall mortality, and to specific markers such as lower risk of disability in activities of daily living and increased frequency of physical activity. Subjective perceptions of health are also affected by meaning in life. Park, Malone, Suresh, Bliss, and Rosen (2008) noted the association of meaning in life with self-perceived quality of life among patients with congestive heart failure.

As a last definitional question, scholars have considered whether meaning is found or made, or both. As noted by Baumeister and Landau (2018), "discovery means finding something that already exists, whereas invention means creating something that did not exist previously" (p. 4). Is meaning in life discovered or found? When the term meaning-making is used, it clearly denotes creating something new. Recall that meaning exists at connections, particularly connections of the known and the unknown. As is clarified in the next section, the creation of meaning includes discrete steps involving cognition and emotions. Thus, for the purposes of this chapter, meaning may be existing but "found," or may also not exist and then "created." This dynamic tension exists throughout any discussion of meaning in life.

Kimberly describes how meaning, including purpose, mattering, and continuity, were affected in her early life and now as an adult.

> I know that because my heart was broken so deeply and so badly, I have a greater level of empathy and compassion for others. I know what it's like to be abused. I know what it's like for your family not to support you, but rather your abuser. I know what it's like to feel completely isolated and alone. I know what it's like to feel as though you have lost yourself, and quite possibly your mind as well. I know what it's like to not be able to eat or sleep, or to escape visions that take over your mind. I know what it's like to feel as though you don't know if you can make it through the next five minutes, let alone the next hour.
>
> Life is a series of seemingly unrelated events that come together to weave the stories of our lives. I know that sometimes we experience a "no" in life but it is only to leave room for a better "yes" to come along down the road. I understand that it is not my job to understand why things happen a certain way, or why they even happen at all. It is down the road that we can look back and have a better understanding of how one event of our life led to another.
>
> From my brokenness, meaning was born. If I am able to use the pain and heartache that I experienced, as well as insights and wisdom I have gained, to help heal or educate another, I absolutely will. Because it's through this pain that I have found my purpose. There is such an immense amount of power to hear "I know" from someone else who has experienced trauma and abuse. There are so many aspects of trauma you experience that words simply don't exist to describe, so to find another soul that understands this without words is so powerful.
>
> Another way I see it is that I didn't choose this life, it chose me. And this may sound crazy, but I believe God called me to use my story to help others. I believe He wants to use what was intended for evil for a greater good. And I have to ask, who am I to question God? Instead I believe I have to trust, and have faith, that if I am called to do something, I will be equipped with what I need.
>
> Life is hard. There are going to be bad things in life and people will make bad choices. We have free will and as humans, we make mistakes in this broken world. This path will not be easy all the time, but it will always be better. You often will have no idea why you're headed in a particular direction but yet you move anyway. It's not until later that things begin to get clear and make a little more sense. But each seemingly small choice we make in life leads to another as our lives are so intricately woven together.

Meaning after trauma

While scholars and clinicians agree on the importance of meaning in life to adjustment and recovery, how meaning influences those outcomes is still unclear.

A comprehensive model for how meaning is disrupted by trauma and is then restored was presented by Park (2010, 2016). In her model, the process begins with global meanings. These meanings are fundamental beliefs about self, about the world, and about the interrelationship between self and world. Some of these global meanings are the core beliefs identified by Janoff-Bulman (1989). The first belief is that the world is a benevolent place, with misfortune, a rare occurrence. The second belief is that life is not random, but has predictability and logic. Believing life has predictability includes the belief that actions under our control affect our outcomes. The last belief is that we are decent and worthwhile. In addition to beliefs, global meanings also contain our goals – desired end states, such as health or achievement – and our subjective sense of mattering.

A second component of Park's model are situational meanings. These meanings are specific to events and situations and are ascribed by the individual, thus containing the individual's subjective interpretation of the event. These situational beliefs may either fit with or contrast to global meanings. As an example, a natural disaster might trigger situational beliefs of its catastrophic nature, uncontrollability, and unfairness. If the individual has global beliefs of benevolence, control, and fairness, these situational beliefs strongly contrast with the global beliefs. That contrast, the inability to accommodate the situation beliefs alongside the global beliefs, is believed to give rise to global meaning violation.

Meaning-making is the term Park uses for efforts by the individual to reduce the emotional distress that accompanies the sharp discrepancy of global and situational beliefs. If that discrepancy is to be reduced or eliminated, either the global beliefs must be changed, or the situational beliefs altered (or both must occur). *Assimilations* are processes that change situational meanings, and *accommodations* are processes that change global beliefs. These processes occur both in emotions and in cognitions. For example, beliefs can be reworked, as might happen when a belief that all life is controllable is modified to include the acknowledgment that some events are outside personal control.

Park's model concludes with meanings made, outcomes of meaning-making in several domains. One domain of meaning made is that an event may come to "make sense" to the individual. A shocking sudden bereavement, for example, may make sense when a loved one's previously unknown medical condition becomes known. A second domain is acceptance, the alteration of the situational belief to become "part of life" rather than being seen as completely alien. A third outcome domain is the creation of positive changes in the person experiencing it. These changes are conceptualized by the term *posttraumatic growth* and include improvements in interpersonal relationships, new directions in life, stronger appreciation of life itself, and newly recognized personal strengths.

Changes in global meanings also are domains of meanings made. Core beliefs may be changed: for example, life may be understood as less fair, less controllable, or less beneficial. Global goals, such as health, may be discarded or altered in important ways. If the individual's global beliefs included a certain view of God or a personal deity, those global beliefs may change. For example, God may be seen as more punishing, or less powerful. An important global meaning change is in the basic sense of "self": the self may be altered to accommodate the new situation, such as happens when a new personal identity is formed (e.g., now I am a "cancer survivor").

Meaning-making attempts following stressful events have been demonstrated to be common. Studies in Park's (2010) review included bereaved parents, individuals paralyzed through accidents, and people living with a chronic health condition: the percentages of people who reported having attempted to make meaning of the experience was typically quite high, as high as 80%. Tallman, Altmaier, and Garcia (2007) studied 90 cancer survivors one year after a stem cell transplant. 91% of those patients had created meaning through identifying benefits from the difficult treatment, the most common of which were significant changes in life perspective and in perceptions of the self.

There are unanswered questions, however, in the model. One such question is whether attempts to find or make meaning always lead to meanings made and then to adjustment. The data are clear that attempts to find meaning are not always successful. As an example, Davis and Morgan (2008) studied persons living with a chronic health condition and found that almost 40% of those studied had failed to find a satisfactory answer to the question of "why me." The data are also clear that great distress can occur from ongoing unsuccessful search for meaning. In a study (Wu et al., 2008) of meaning-making and adjustment to bereavement among mothers of deceased children, mothers still searching for meaning three months after their child's death experienced more distress than mothers who reported finding meaning.

A second unanswered question is whether some meanings are more helpful than others. Are meanings interchangeable in their influence on the adjustment process? Data from adult earthquake survivors (Feder et al., 2013) provided important information for this question. Those survivors three years after the earthquake who had a higher sense of purpose in life reported fewer depressive symptoms. In contrast, those survivors who believed they had been punished or abandoned by God experienced more negative emotions, even among persons who reported finding meaning in life. In this sample, therefore, certain global beliefs were associated with a less favorable outcome even in the context of finding meaning.

A third unanswered question is the duration of the meaning-making and meaning-made process. It is difficult for researchers to definitely answer this question, partially because the ways in which this question is answered has varied among studies between sense-making and benefit-finding. Davis, Wortman, Lehman, and Silver (2000) studied over 200 bereaved adults who lost children to Sudden Infant Death Syndrome (SIDS) or lost a child or spouse in a motor vehicle accident. Their data revealed that fewer participants were able to find meaning over a delayed time, a result contradicting the notion that finding meaning is more likely as extended time passes. In fact, the authors concluded that if the bereaved in their study were able to find meaning, they did so relatively quickly after the loss.

Kimberly wrote about how meaning was affected and made after her trauma.

My paternal grandma who was "my person" died just a year prior to the exposure of Mike's sexual deviances. She was diagnosed and died within a month. And there's something to be said for how she lived her life fully up until the end, and faded quickly. I remember thinking at the time how quickly my grandma had died; to be diagnosed and dead within a month was crazy, but also the timing of it. She had fought multiple cancers, had heart attacks like they were nothing, and then to die so quickly. I knew something was up with that but I also knew that this was something I would not understand until later. But a year later, upon my stepdad's arrest, I did find meaning in why she died when she did. If there was one person in this world who would have gone to the ends of the earth to protect me it would have been her. I remember my uncle even commenting about knowing why my grandma and my dad had both already died, as they would have hardly thought about it before they inflicted harm on Mike for what he did to me, and then we would be left with another mess. And although I know she would not have asked, to have to explain how I didn't tell her would have been horrible to face as well.

But also, bigger picture, having my grandma walk alongside me as my angel was a far greater gift than I ever could have imagined. In the worst moments of my life I called to God to show me the way. And then I called upon my dad and grandma to walk alongside me when I couldn't walk. Many times, they carried me. I know they did. It was a huge benefit to have my grandma as my angel at that time. Though it still hurt and tore my heart to pieces, I understood and could find greater meaning in it.

This past Spring I started a class at our church called WalkWithMe in which we journey together on the road to becoming a survivor. I believe with the support of other survivors we can not only survive but also learn how to thrive this side of trauma. Alongside the class, I've hosted an event called Supporting a Survivor in which professionals such as detectives, university police, advocates, a prosecutor, and a nurse sat on a panel as we educated how to best walk alongside a survivor of sexual violence. The WalkWithMe class and Supporting a Survivor event has been hosted at two of our church campuses so far! I am currently working on how to incorporate this into a larger program to better meet the needs of our community. Most recently I have started to speak in a more informational, training type situation, utilizing my own story as well as all the information and insights I've learned and experienced about trauma along the way. So much freedom can come from knowledge and understanding, so if I can share what I have learned and help people connect with it through my personal account I absolutely will.

At the end of the day, I'm just a normal person and I always find myself saying, "I'm just me." I'm a wife and mother. It felt uncomfortable at first, especially not growing up with church myself. I thought "oh great, I've become one of those religious freaks." Fact is, I would not be where I am today without God taking the wheel. Just a short four years ago, I never in my wildest dreams would have imagined my life looking as it does now. And quite honestly, I have no idea what is to come, I am simply following where this path leads. I know that without God guiding me through these last four years I most certainly would not be where I am today. I just wouldn't be. It is only from my own willingness to learn more about how God communicates with us and guides and leads us, and having the courage to trust that He knows what the grand plan is, that any of this have been brought to life. I have been called into doing many things I am not naturally comfortable doing, but yet, I just have to believe that there is a greater meaning to it and hope that it will make sense as I look back later. I know with all my heart that God does not cause evil, but He most definitely can overcome evil and instead bring light into where darkness once was.

Promoting meaning

How is meaning-making initiated, maintained, and mastered? There are few interventions to promote meaning-making in clinical literature, although some have been designed and evaluated. For example, *life review* was an intervention originally designed for use with the elderly to promote achievement of an integrated and acceptable understanding of one's life (see Butler, 1974), particularly in the presence of mild to moderate depression. It has been used in a variety of ways since then, with the intended purpose of promoting hope and life satisfaction.

The focus of this text is on clinicians promoting positive strengths among clients in order to enhance their effectiveness during life after trauma. Therefore, discussing the ways in which clients have meaning in their life, and the ways in which that meaning or those meanings were affected by the trauma is critical. How can the client's sense of purpose, value, and direction be mobilized in the face of significant adversity?

There are certainly practical behaviors for cultivating meaning. Baumeister and Landau (2018) noted the straightforward characteristic of meaning as its connectivity. Thus, meaning is fostered by integration. The present must be integrated with the past, and that connection in turn modifies the present and its connection to the future. A process of obtaining that connection is expressive writing such as might occur in a journal. Boals (2012) considered the outcomes of expressive writing for 84 participants after they experienced a negative event. In her study, participants who wrote about highly stressful events and who evidenced increased meaning-making over three sessions of writing were less distressed.

Another way to foster meaning is to highlight its commonplace role in our lives rather than its appearance during trauma. Heintzelman and King (2014) were among the first to document meaning in life evidenced in a range of large-scale surveys. Their data revealed that, overall, most people find their lives to be meaningful, including individuals facing challenging experiences. Finding meaning in an admittedly imperfect world includes occasional failures to understand or connect as well as opportunities to appreciate rather than understand.

Religiousness and spirituality is the topic of the next chapter, but the relationship of these beliefs and values are, for some persons, central to their meaning-making. For these clients, exploring the contributions of their beliefs, whether as a facilitator or a barrier of meaning-making, is important. In a study of survivors of Hurricane Katrina (Haynes et al., 2017), the degree to which spiritual meaning attenuated the loss of resources was considered. Among these survivors, those who reported finding greater spiritual meaning suffered less than survivors who found less spiritual meaning, even when experiencing considerable loss.

Kimberly considered ways to increase meaning-making in her own life and in the lives of others.

I think to maximize the experience of using your story to help others, it is helpful to make sure that what you're doing aligns with your natural gifts and talents. In my own experience, I plugged in wherever someone needed help. In the beginning, this involved speaking different places on various aspects of my story. Some have asked me to speak on a specific topic while others have also asked me to go more in depth on my story and discuss the victimology of it all, leaving a longer amount of time to field questions.

I will be the first to say that I am not a public speaker. I am not polished nor am I smooth-sounding and scripted. I have had various people come up to me after speaking and tell me they felt as though I was talking right to them, and we were having a personal conversation. The funny thing is that when I see polished, motivational speakers, they seem really good to me. I sit back and think to myself that I do not compare to them at all, nor do I have near the amount of skill they possess. Similar to speaking, is my ability to write. I have said a number of times, as people have suggested I write a book, that I am not a writer.

I have said that I am not a public speaker, nor am I writer. Perhaps this is not exactly accurate. I guess I was looking at it through the lens of your traditional speakers and writers. I have come to learn that I can only speak and write straight from my heart, bringing full, raw emotion and delivering in this conversational style. What is most interesting is that is how I have always been, as evident as early as age 11 when my grandpa died. So instead of arguing that I cannot speak publicly and that I am not a writer, if I use my God given gifts and talents, I in fact can do just that.

Another example of this is recently leading a class for survivors of sexual abuse and sexual assault. I did not have it all mapped out and know exactly what I was doing, yet I was able to create a very powerful and impactful class. And again, looking back, I used to want to be a teacher, then a professor. I've always gotten good reviews as a teaching assistant and at leading discussion groups. So again, I was able to succeed using my story to help others because I was utilizing my gifts and talents.

This summer a dear friend of mine shared a very helpful insight with me. As we were discussing spiritual gifts she told me that she had found if you utilize your spiritual gifts you will feel rejuvenated and energized by your work, while if you're operating outside of them you may feel drained. I have found this to be true time and time again. When you step back and take inventory of where your interests lie and what gifts and talents you possess, figuring out how to create meaning from your trauma will become clearer. Using your story to help others is incredibly powerful, but not always easy. I often question my ability and lack confidence. If you are utilizing skills and talents in which you are confident, it can help make this transition to making meaning from your trauma easier. It will not be easy, but using the gifts and talents you already possess can make it more natural and more likely come across more authentic as well.

Summary

Meaning in life is made or discovered through connections. Trauma, however, occurs through violation of the connections individuals have to ordinary systems of care and support. One strength that must be promoted after trauma is meaning-making. Meaning includes comprehension, purpose, and mattering, which are distinct aspects of meaning. Each of these aspects can be affected in a positive way through making sense of trauma, identifying benefits, and creating connections from past to future.

References

Baumeister, R. F., & Landau, M. J. (2018). Finding the meaning of meaning: Emerging insights on four grand questions. *Review of General Psychology*, *22*, 1–10.

Boals, A. (2012). The use of meaning making in expressive writing: When meaning is beneficial. *Journal of Social and Clinical Psychology*, *31*, 393–409.

Butler, R. N. (1974). Successful aging and the role of life review. *Journal of the American Geriatrics Society*, *22*, 529–535.

Davis, C. G., & Morgan, M. S. (2008). Finding meaning, perceiving growth, and acceptance of tinnitus. *Rehabilitation Psychology*, *53*, 128–138.

Davis, C. G., Wortman, C. B., Lehman, D. R., & Silver, R. C. (2000). Searching for meaning in loss: Are clinical assumptions correct? *Death Studies*, *24*, 497–540.

Feder, A., Ahmad, S., Lee, E. J., Morgan, J. E., Singh, R., Smith, B. W., ... Charney, D. S. (2013). Coping and PTSD symptoms in Pakistani earthquake survivors: Purpose in life, religious coping, and social support. *Journal of Affective Disorders*, *147*, 156–163.

Frankl, V. E. (1963). *Man's search for meaning: An introduction to logotherapy*. Oxford, UK: Washington Square Press.

George, L. S., & Park, C. L. (2017). The multidimensional existential meaning scale: A tripartite approach to measuring meaning in life. *The Journal of Positive Psychology*, *12*, 613–627.

Haynes, W. C., Van Tongeren, D. R., Aten, J., Davis, E. B., Davis, D. E., Hook, J. N., ... Johnson, T. (2017). The meaning as buffer hypothesis: Spiritual meaning attenuates the effect of disaster-related resource loss on posttraumatic stress. *Psychology of Religion and Spirituality*, *9*, 446–453.

Heintzelman, S. J., & King, L. A. (2014). Life is pretty meaningful. *American Psychologist*, *69*, 561–574.

Ho, M. Y., Cheung, F. M., & Cheung, S. F. (2010). The role of meaning in life and optimism in promoting well-being. *Personality and Individual Differences*, *48*, 658–663.

Hooker, S. A., Masters, K. S., & Park, C. L. (2018). A meaningful life is a healthy life: A conceptual model linking meaning and meaning salience to health. *Review of General Psychology*, *22*, 11–24.

Janoff-Bulman, R. (1989). Assumptive worlds and the stress of traumatic events: Applications of the scheme concept. *Social Cognition*, *7*, 113–136.

Lindy, J. D. (2006). Mutative transference and the restoration of the posttraumatic self. In J. P. Wilson (Ed.), *The posttraumatic self: Restoring meaning and wholeness to personality* (pp. 295–332). New York, NY: Routledge.

Park, C. L. (2010). Making sense of the meaning literature: An integrative review of meaning making and its effects on adjustment to stressful life events. *Psychological Bulletin*, *136*, 257–301.

Park, C. L. (2016). Meaning making in the context of disasters. *Journal of Clinical Psychology*, *72*, 1234–1246.

Park, C. L., Malone, M. R., Suresh, D. P., Bliss, D., & Rosen, R. I. (2008). Coping, meaning in life, and quality of life in congestive heart failure patients. *Quality of Life Research: An International Journal of Quality of Life Aspects of Treatment, Care & Rehabilitation*, *17*, 21–26.

Roepke, A. M., Jayawickreme, E., & Riffle, O. M. (2014). Meaning and health: A systematic review. *Applied Research in Quality of Life*, *9*, 1055–1079.

Ryff, C. D. (1989). Happiness is everything or is it? Explorations on the meaning of psychological well-being. *Journal of Personality and Social Psychology*, *57*, 1069–1081.
Seligman, M. E. P. (February 24, 2017). *The PERMA model: Your scientific theory of happiness*. Available from https://positivepsychologyprogram.com/perma-model/.
Steger, M. F. (2009). Meaning in life. In S. J. Lopez, & C. R. Snyder (Eds.), *Oxford handbook of positive psychology* (2nd ed., pp. 679–687). New York, NY: Oxford University Press.
Steger, M. F., Kashdan, T. B., Sullivan, B. A., & Lorentz, D. (2008). Understanding the search for meaning in life: Personality, cognitive style, and the dynamic between seeking and experiencing meaning. *Journal of Personality*, *76*, 199–228.
Tallman, B. A., Altmaier, E. M., & Garcia, C. (2007). Finding benefit from cancer. *Journal of Counseling Psychology*, *54*, 481–487.
Wu, L., Bonanno, G., DuHamel, K., Redd, W. H., Rini, C., Austin, J., ... Manne, S. (2008). Pre-bereavement meaning and post-bereavement distress in mothers of children who underwent haematopoietic stem cell transplantation. *British Journal of Health Psychology*, *13*, 419–433.

Resources for clinicians and clients

Altmaier, E. M. (Ed.), (2017). *Reconstructing meaning after trauma: Theory, research, and practice*. San Diego, CA: Academic Press.
Garland, J., & Garland, C. (2001). *Life review in health and social care*. New York, NY: Routledge.
Hill, C. E. (2018). *Meaning in life: A therapist's guide*. Washington, DC: American Psychological Association.
Landau, M. J. (2017). *Finding meaning in an imperfect world*. New York, NY: Oxford University Press.
Landau, M. J. (2018). Using metaphor to find meaning in life. *Review of General Psychology*, *22*, 62–72.
Park, C. L., Currier, J. M., Harris, J. I., & Slattery, J. M. (2017). *Trauma, meaning, and spirituality: Translating research into clinical practice*. Washington, DC: American Psychological Association.

Religiousness and spirituality

8

Psychology has had an ambivalent relationship with matters of religious faith and spiritual experience. Early psychologists were sincerely interested in these topics, such as William James' treatise on religious experience (James, 1902). However, during development of a more "scientific" approach to scholarship and toward an emphasis on the pathological, psychology entered a period of decades where scholarship on religiousness and spirituality was relegated to the minority and the experience of religious faith and spirituality was somewhat pathologized (see Pruyser, 1971). Within the positive psychology movement, however, came a reinvigoration of interest in the role and function of universal experiences of religiousness and spirituality.

In many ways, meaning-making is a component part of the positive processes of religiousness and spirituality. As noted by Park, Currier, Harris, and Slattery (2017), all major world religions have defined components of meaning in life. For example, religions have defined essential purposes of life, and contrasted trajectories of failure and redemption. However, as Chapter 7 describes, meaning exists apart from religiously defined meaning. Likewise, the influence of religiousness and spirituality occurs outside of the strength of meaning. Therefore, this chapter considers how the positive processes of religiousness and spirituality foster recovery after trauma, including but also extending from their influence in meaning-making.

It should be noted that a significant literature on religiousness and spirituality exists outside of positive psychology, and therefore many important topics will not be covered in this chapter. The interested readers are encouraged to consult reviews (e.g., Emmons & Paloutzian, 2003) and handbooks (e.g., Pargament, 2013). This chapter considers how religiousness and spirituality operate within and after trauma, as well as ways in which they can be promoted. In this chapter, too, are Kimberly's responses to the following definitions and questions:

Religiousness definition

A commitment to and beliefs about God or a deity that create a framework for life, participation in individual religious behaviors (such as prayer), and participation in a community of like-minded persons and in their collective practices (such as worship, teaching, learning); adherence to organizational beliefs and practices.

Spirituality definition

The deep experience of connectedness to the transcendent and sacred; having personal experiences of things of the spirit (different from material or worldly interests), the ongoing union of values and passions with activities related to ultimate significance.

Promoting Positive Processes after Trauma. DOI: https://doi.org/10.1016/B978-0-12-811975-4.00008-3
Copyright © 2019 Elsevier Inc. and Kimberly Gleason. All rights reserved.

Religiousness and spirituality questions

When did you begin to see that your life experiences, including those of trauma, related to your religiousness and/or spirituality? How did that change over time, if it did change over time?
Speaking more directly to religiousness, how have you incorporated your traumatic life experiences into your religious beliefs and practices?
Speaking more directly to spirituality, how have you incorporated your traumatic life experiences into your spiritual experiences and practice?
Has your sense of God changed over time? How do you see your sense of God as being the same as, and different from, others you know who do not have your life experiences?
What might help someone else in your situation find religiousness and spirituality to be beneficial in promoting meaning in life?
How has your personal involvement in religiousness and spirituality created a faith-infused framework for your life?

Defining religiousness and spirituality

Research and clinical scholarship on religiousness and spirituality is replete with confusing, duplicative, or contradictory definitions. Harris, Howell, and Spurgeon (2018) reviewed an extensive body of published work to determine common factors of religiousness and spirituality as proposed by professionals. They used definitional content analysis, examining over 500 publications to specify research-based definitions to guide future research and clinical practice, and found discernable characteristics that differentiated religiousness from spirituality. Spirituality was characterized as follows:

Internal emphasis. Experiences encompassed within spirituality are primarily those of an internal nature (e.g., state of being) that create a sense of peace and fulfillment.

Ultimate concerns. Spirituality concerns itself with values and purposes larger and more unifying than those of everyday life.

Self-enhancement. Growth occurs through an individualized connection between heart and mind and between oneself and the natural world.

In contrast, religiousness was characterized as follows:

Beliefs. The focus of religiousness is understanding and adhering to sets of beliefs—about the nature of the divine, about the nature of humans, and about the interaction of the divine with humans.

Rituals. Religiousness involves participation in a culture that proclaims the value of certain private and communal rituals.

Behaviors. The practice of religiousness is characterized by actions that are seen to fulfill codes of ethics and values as well as to provide charity (love) to others inside and outside the faith group.

An early attempt to delineate these constructs among non-professionals using community-living adults who responded to an online survey (Gall, Malette, &

Guirguis-Younger, 2011) revealed moderate agreement about concepts of spirituality and religiousness. Spirituality was defined by a series of themes: core self (the centrality of the deepest part of the "self"), life perspective, relationship with God or higher power, a sense of mystery, and a connection to the world. Religiousness, in contrast, was defined as: participation in an organization or system, beliefs about God or a higher power, moral and ethical proscriptions, and a pathway to achieve spirituality.

For the purposes of this chapter, *religiousness* is defined as a commitment to and beliefs about God or a deity that create a meaning framework, promote participation in religious behaviors both individual and corporate, and motivate adherence to organizational beliefs and practices. *Spirituality* is defined as deep experience of connectedness to the transcendent or sacred, personal experiences of spiritual interests, and activities related to ultimate significance.

In the aggregate, spirituality involves individual, experiential, connective associations and religiousness involves individual and group, belief-based, ritually rich, practices. It is important context for this chapter that today, in the United States, there is a demarcation of people into four groups (see Lipka & Gecewicz, 2017): 27% of adults think of themselves as "spiritual but not religious," 48% as "both spiritual and religious," 6% as "religious but not spiritual," and 18% as "neither religious nor spiritual." As the authors noted, membership in the category of "spiritual but not religious" has increased over the past decade primarily as membership in "both religious and spiritual" has fallen.

Here are Kimberly's memories of and current perspectives on religiousness and spirituality.

> Spirituality for me can best be understood by my relationship with God. For me, the higher being in life is God. I do understand that others believe in a higher being and do not call it God. I think believing in someone or something bigger than yourself is a critical piece to recovery. If you do not believe in a higher power, I am not sure how you can get through trauma. I tell victims I meet, as they journey to survivor, that no human can take their pain away and make things better. I believe this. It takes something bigger than ourselves to overcome such evil.
>
> As a child I would pray at night, without knowing that's what I was doing. I guess I thought I was talking to God, but I had no concept of what or who God was. I would lean on God through the life challenges I faced as a young child. I did not know how to process or understand my dad having a heart attack when I was only three years old, knowing he could die. It's very hard to love openly after experiencing the possibility of such loss, even for an adult let alone a child. I did not understand how my parents could get divorced, and now my dad was gone except for every other weekend. How can a child make sense of these things without relying on a higher power?
>
> I think people get hung up on religion and the act of being religious. They go to church, sometimes just on holidays. They pray, they live righteously, and they don't swear. The greatest blessing in my life is my spiritual connection with God. Again, if you cannot call it God, call it what you want, but I believe this spiritual piece is so vital. And at the end of the day, we're all talking about the same thing, and to me, it's God. That higher connection, knowing that there is something more, that there is more to this life than ourselves and something that transcends our circumstance. It is this spiritual connection that drives and motivates me to find a greater meaning in life.

Religiousness and spirituality after trauma

It is not uncommon to find survivors of trauma expressing spiritual or religious struggles or doubts since global beliefs touch on deeply existential matters, even if the person is not explicitly "religious." As noted by Park et al. (2017), most persons experience trauma as an assault on their basic beliefs about human existence, suffering, and identity, and these basic beliefs are essentially spiritual and religious concerns. There is evidence, as well, that suffering provokes questions of the role of a deity in life. "Where was God while this was happening" is a common response to misfortune and pain, and nonbenevolent explanations are that God is revealed in the occurrence of trauma to be weak, punitive, malevolent, or uninvolved (see beliefs about suffering; Wilt, Exline, Grubbs, Park, & Pargament, 2016).

One of the interesting aspects of trauma's effects on religiousness is that trauma has been shown to create both increase and decrease in religiosity. ter Kuile and Ehring (2014) studied 300 survivors regarding changes in their religious beliefs and practices after traumas ranging from personally experienced violence to sudden and unexpected death of or injury to a loved one. Of the sample, 50% reported no change in religiousness, and the remainder were equally split between a decrease and an increase. Of interest, those participants who reported a greater sense that their personal assumptions were violated were more likely to have a decrease in religious beliefs and practices.

Certainly undergoing shattered assumptions about benevolence or a just deity is one explanation for erosion of the processes of religiousness and spirituality. Another explanation is that persons may cope with trauma effects through a range of responses labeled as religious coping. Religious coping (see Pargament, Koenig, & Perez, 2000) is complex in nature, and may be facilitative or debilitating. One function of religious coping is to gain a new perspective on the trauma through reorientation: "I thought the trauma might bring me closer to God" and "I realized there are some things that even God cannot change." Another function is to gain control over an uncontrollable situation: "I tried to make sense of the situation" creates more control than "I pleaded with God to work everything out." The last function is to gain comfort and closeness to others: "I asked for support from others" versus "I wondered if God had given up on me."

The role of the spiritual struggle itself was examined by Evans et al. (2018) among a sample of veterans, some of whom suffered a moral injury in combat through direct or observed violation of deeply held beliefs and values. Also assessed were symptoms of distress, including depression and post-traumatic stress disorder symptoms. For veterans reporting morally injurious events, spiritual and religious struggles were associated with later anxiety and depression.

This chapter considers both religiousness and spirituality, although research evaluating the influence of trauma on both of these processes is less common than research evaluating results on religiousness. Lee, Park, and Hale (2016) surveyed college students regarding their experience of potentially traumatic events and a range of religious and spiritual beliefs and practices. Their findings documented that traumas did affect some aspects of religiousness and spirituality (e.g., belief in God, experience of religious comfort), but did not affect other aspects (e.g., corporate religious practices, seeing God as benevolent). Thus, there is not an uniform way in which trauma acts on the many dimensions of religiousness and spirituality, which suggests both a need to be thorough in its exploration with clients as well as the opportunity for a range of processes to be promoted.

Children and adolescents, as well as adults, experience trauma in their lives, and the influence of positive processes is important for them as well. This consideration particularly applies to the influence of religiousness and spirituality in childhood and adolescence. It is not the case that adult development is necessary for a sense of spiritual connection or the articulation of beliefs about God or a deity. Fowler (1981) first presented a model of faith development that relied on the developmental psychology of Piaget and proposed defined stages of faith, beginning with an intuitive faith in the preschool child. Sequential stages were mythic-literal faith, conventional faith, and reflective faith.

Trauma creates challenges to religiousness and spirituality among children and adolescents even though their faith may not have the same structure as among adults. Bryant-Davis et al. (2012) considered those challenges. Parallel to the experience of adults, young people have difficulty reconciling their beliefs with their traumatic experiences, believe that God is punishing them for their behavior, and feel a sense of shame or guilt. In a recent study, Boynston (2017) used qualitative methods to construct a theoretical model of children's spirituality after trauma, grief, and loss. Her data revealed that children experienced spiritual lives, with beliefs and practices. However, trauma caused children to engage in questions and doubt. This struggle, unfortunately, was "navigated in seclusion", since the children did not believe that their distress would be socially validated and did not know how or with whom to share it.

One particular trauma deserves special mention, betrayal trauma in the context of a faith-informed relationship (see Birrell, Bernstein, and Freyd (2017) for a presentation of betrayal trauma). Abuse or maltreatment by trusted religious or spiritual figures is uniquely victimizing for children and adolescents. Martin, Van Ryzin, and Dishion (2016) examined profiles of response among adolescents after a range of traumas during childhood, including betrayal traumas. Adolescents after betrayal trauma were more likely to have major psychiatric disorders and severe emotional distress. The outcomes of this trauma are debilitating and long-lasting, and include damaged spiritual and religious systems of belief and connection (Walker, Courtois, & Aten, 2015).

Here are Kimberly's considerations of how her sense of religiousness and spirituality were affected by her traumas.

I believe I first experienced God when my paternal grandpa died around age 11. My grandma had hired me that summer to care for grandpa as he was dying instead of babysitting neighborhood kids as I usually did. As I cared for him, we shared many conversations and a lot of time together. When it came to the day he died, I saw the wonder of God. They had called my mom early that afternoon to say things weren't looking good and to come over if we wanted to say goodbye. It took me a couple of hours to work up the nerve to go over to their house. When I arrived, it took another decent amount of time, probably a half hour or forty-five minutes, to work up the nerve to walk down the hallway to the bedroom where my grandpa lay in bed with his breaths getting slower and weaker. When I came into the room all his closest family was there. No sooner had I muttered the words "good bye grandpa, I love you" than he took that final breath, his head turned to the side, and his body became completely relaxed and at peace. I know he waited for me.

From this experience with my grandpa, I came to believe that in some circumstances, especially when someone is terminally ill, God may allow a little more time to tie up loose ends on Earth. So then about eight years later when my dad died, I struggled. I had gotten a call that he was wasn't doing well but I was an hour away at a training session. Once back in town while I waited for my brother to get back as well, I went to grab some fast-food and came back to my mom's house. When I returned, food in hand, I saw the look on my mom's face and knew instantly. My dad had died before I made it up to the hospital to say that final goodbye. I felt awful, like I left him waiting there too long.

One night that year as I was having a bad night and struggling with a friend about the loss of my dad, I remember her turning to look at me and asking if I had ever thought about the idea that maybe he didn't want me there. I had never thought of it that way until then. But that all made complete sense and I knew as soon as she spoke the words that she was right. How could my dad have said goodbye and left with any sort of peace knowing he was leaving his 19-year-old daughter and 22-year-old son without their dad? I don't think he would have been able to leave in peace.

My spiritual connection has helped me find a greater purpose for the pain I went through with my sexual abuse, the exposure of it, and how my family handled it. It is this strong spiritual connection that has guided me along a path to uncover ways to plug in and use the wisdom and insights I learned through my trauma to help others. An example of this is a class I recently created called WalkWithMe. The idea came from the fact that I felt God walking with me, guiding me, and placing others in my life to help me journey from being a victim to becoming a survivor. I believe that no human can take the pain away, and the best they can do is walk alongside you. Just as I believe that people were placed in my life to walk alongside me through the worst season of my life, I can now utilize what I have learned to walk alongside others. As others experience the power of this companionship, they too are inspired and motivated to help others recover as well. The power of the Spirit, and the ability to connect with others, is a power so strong and undeniable that it can help people transcend their circumstance and move from being a victim to becoming a survivor.

Promoting religiousness and spirituality

The provision of meaning has been identified as one central contribution of religiousness and spirituality. George and Park (2017) studied 300 adults diagnosed with and treated for heart failure or for cancer over a 1-year time period. Patients with higher spirituality at the initial time point, compared to patients with lower spirituality, reported more positive changes in meaning making at the 1-year follow-up. That this relationship held across two types of diseases (progressively worsening vs. progressively improving) was an especially robust finding and suggests that spirituality serves as a positive process through its facilitation of meaning-making.

However, spirituality has a complex relationship with meaning-making. A qualitative study of the relationship of spirituality with meaning among adult patients diagnosed with and treated for cancer (Uwland-Sikkema, Visser, Westerhof, & Garssen, 2018) determined four categories of spirituality present within meaning-making systems. The first was a pervasive spirituality influencing meaning. These participants set meaning as a first priority, and spirituality as their responsibility to maintain through practices such as prayer, yoga, and meditation. The second was spirituality influencing meaning through personal characteristics, such as optimism and energy. The third were participants who assumed personal responsibility for their lives, and spirituality was a less articulated aspect of self. Last were interviewees who appeared to have meaning systems devoid of spiritual meanings.

Harper and Pargament (2015) identified four specific ways in which religiousness and spirituality serve as a positive process after trauma other than through meaning-making: conferring mastery or control, receiving support from others, experiencing connectedness with the divine, and creating a transformative perspective. For example, Bryant-Davis (2005) studied adult survivors of childhood trauma and found that spirituality influenced coping through a new belief that justice would apply—the perpetrator would have to answer to God even if justice was not attained directly by the victim. Among refugees interviewed by Hussain and Bhushan (2011), Buddhism was a positive resource for coping by providing historical role models of strength in adversity.

Parallel with adults, young people use trauma as a stimulus for posttraumatic growth and other personal enduring changes. Meyerson, Grant, Carter, and Kilmer (2011) reviewed evidence that posttraumatic growth occurs among adolescents after trauma, and that religiosity is positively associated with growth. One component of posttraumatic growth is the new directions, such as turning to helping others of similar circumstances. At the time of the writing of this text, for example, students who survived the Marjory Stoneman Douglas High School shootings were engaged in advocacy for changes in gun control laws (see http://www.chicagotribune.com/news/nationworld/ct-florida-students-gun-laws-20180216-story.html)

Another way in which religiousness and spirituality can serve as a positive process is in their contribution to *spiritual transformation*. This concept has a long tradition in mysticism both Christian and Buddhist, and was originally seen as primarily experiential and achieved only over a long journey. Pargament (2006) introduced the idea of spiritual transformation as a fundamental change in life of the place of the sacred or the divine. That transformation presumably is for increased importance, when the spiritual or sacred assumes a more central role. However, an early study (Cole, Hopkins, Tisak, Steel, & Carr, 2008) found that patients with cancer demonstrated acceleration in both the importance of spirituality and the loss of importance. They termed the former "spiritual growth" and the latter, "spiritual decline." Among those patients studied, spiritual growth was associated with well-being, while spiritual decline was associated with emotional distress.

In contrast to other positive processes, the role of religiousness can be dual-edged. As Pargament (2002) notes, psychology has tended to view religiousness as global processes that are largely beneficial (or largely harmful). In contrast, he notes that religiousness can have both positive and negative influences, depending in part on the person (e.g., how well is religiousness integrated into the personality) or the situation (certain types of religious coping seem to result in more difficulties). Pargament argues for a certain approach to religiousness and spirituality that parallels that of a positive process: that approach is "internalized, intrinsically motivated, and built on a belief in a greater meaning in life" (p. 177).

In support of that assertion, Barton and Miller (2015) conducted a survey among 4000 adolescents and young adults regarding their spiritual experiences and several positive processes (e.g., meaning, forgiveness). Among the participants, high levels of spirituality coincided with high levels of positive processes, and both were associated with reduced depression. Further, personal spirituality was protective against substance abuse. The authors concluded that perhaps spirituality served as a foundation for the operation of other positive processes.

Kimberly writes of her activities and experiences in this positive process.

I believe getting things on paper is a great window into your heart, especially when you learn the art of not filtering your thoughts. I have always been one to journal when life gets rough. I returned to journaling shortly after everything was exposed with my stepdad. One of the neat things about journaling is when you can go back and read your writing later and get insight on yourself and your perspective that you didn't realize at the time. I experienced this very thing when I looked back at my journaling and found that on September 4, 2014, just five days following Mike's arrest, I had dropped into prayer unknowingly while writing.

Thursday, September 4, 2014

God help me, give me the strength and the courage to follow through with this. Please provide as much protection and a sense of safety through this. Thank you for the courage to finally admit this to myself and my closest loved ones. It really has started to bring a sense of moving towards healing-it was good to unlock it from inside of me. I know that good things take greater effort, and the best thing is rarely the easiest.

Help me to remember that it's not my fault regardless what blame others try to lay. That fact is so easily forgotten. It does really hurt to know loved ones will likely still stand by and support him, and then in turn I'll feel as though they don't believe me. Not that I want him to be alone and feel horrible, I don't. I know he will need more love and support to make it through this. It just likely cannot be from me! That's too much!

Maybe someday I'll find peace, and forgiveness will overcome my heart. I really do just want to move forward and begin to put this mess back together. I guess first we need to know what all pieces we're playing with.

Please Lord, please-help me. I need strength. Dad, Grandma-can you help me? I love you, and miss you. Thank you, God, for bringing goodness and an opportunity to grow out of this. Maybe some greater healing will come from this much larger mess.

I love you, Thank you.

Amen

My religion and spirituality created a solid faith-infused framework for my life. One of the greatest benefits I recently realized was the ability to let go and believe. I no longer feel I need to have control over my life and to always know what is coming and what is next. I have such a strong spiritual connection to God now that I am able to trust and let go of that control. I find great freedom in not knowing things now. I have accepted that I am on a need-to-know basis with God, and sometimes things just are not for me to know.

I have been plugging in and finding various ways to use my story to bring healing to others. The way I see it is that I did not choose to have this story, nor did I choose for it to be exposed as it was. But I do now get to choose what to do with it. And coupled that with the fact that my abuser is dead, I have great freedom. I did not have to see him stand trial, and I did not have to testify against him as my mom's family chose to support him. I don't have to worry about when he gets out of jail, or if I may run into him, or worse yet, if he's still offending other victims. I am free. And I believe that by relying on my spiritual relationship I now have with God, He will equip me, and I can use my trauma to help others.

Summary

Religiousness and spirituality are two strengths that are related but not overlapping, and create a variety of positive consequences for the individual after trauma. Meaning-making is the most obvious of those consequences, and is critical for resolving the discrepancy of beliefs and events. However, religiousness and spirituality also foster a sense of companionship and support, both with others and with the divine. Rituals, either alone or in a group, provide a means of grieving, storytelling, and reconstruction of self. Both of these positive processes have been shown to increase physical and psychological well-being, and so have both immediate and delayed benefit for the survivor.

References

Barton, Y. A., & Miller, L. (2015). Spirituality and positive psychology go hand in hand: An investigation of multiple empirically derived profiles and related protective benefits. *Journal of Religion and Health*, *54*, 829–843.

Birrell, P. J., Bernstein, R. E., & Freyd, J. J. (2017). With the fierce and loving embrace of another's soul: Finding connection and meaning after the profound disconnection of betrayal trauma. In E. M. Altmaier (Ed.), *Reconstructing meaning after trauma: Theory, research, and practice* (pp. 29–46). New York, NY: Elsevier.

Boynston, H. M. (2017). Navigating in seclusion: The complicated terrain of children's spirituality in trauma, grief and loss. *Dissertation Abstracts International*, *78*, 5-A(E).

Bryant-Davis, T. (2005). Coping strategies of African American adult survivors of childhood violence. *Professional Psychology: Research and Practice*, *36*, 409–414.

Bryant-Davis, T., Ellis, M. U., Burke-Maynard, E., Moon, N., Counts, P. A., & Anderson, G. (2012). Religiosity, spirituality, and trauma recovery in the lives of children and adolescents. *Professional Psychology: Research & Practice*, *43*, 306–314.

Cole, B. S., Hopkins, C. M., Tisak, J., Steel, J. L., & Carr, B. I. (2008). Assessing spiritual growth and spiritual decline following a diagnosis of cancer: Reliability and validity of the spiritual transformation scale. *Psycho-Oncology*, *17*, 112–121.

Emmons, R. A., & Paloutzian, R. F. (2003). The psychology of religion. *Annual Review of Psychology*, *54*, 377–402.

Evans, W. R., Stanley, M. A., Barrera, T. L., Exline, J. J., Pargament, K. I., & Teng, E. J. (2018). Morally injurious events and psychological distress among veterans: Examining the mediating role of religious and spiritual struggles. *Psychological Trauma: Theory, Research, Practice, and Policy*, *10*, 360–367.

Fowler, J. (1981). *Stages of faith*. San Francisco, CA: Harper and Row.

Gall, T. L., Malette, J., & Guirguis-Younger, M. (2011). Spirituality and religiousness: A diversity of definitions. *Journal of Spirituality in Mental Health*, *13*, 158–181.

George, L. S., & Park, C. L. (2017). Does spirituality confer meaning in life among heart failure patients and cancer survivors? *Psychology of Religion and Spirituality*, *9*, 131–136.

Harper, A. R., & Pargament, K. I. (2015). Trauma, religion, and spirituality: Pathways to healing. In K. E. Cherry (Ed.), *Traumatic stress and long-term recovery* (pp. 349–367). Basil, Switzerland: Springer International Publishing.

Harris, K. A., Howell, D. S., & Spurgeon, D. W. (2018). Faith concepts in psychology: Three 30-year definitional content analyses. *Psychology of Religion and Spirituality*, *10*, 1–29.

Hussain, D., & Bhushan, B. (2011). Cultural factors promoting coping among Tibetan refugees: A qualitative investigation. *Mental Health, Religion & Culture*, *14*, 575–587.

James, W. (1902). *The varieties of religious experience: A study in human nature*. London, UK: Longmans, Green and Co.

Lee, S. Y., Park, C. L., & Hale, A. E. (2016). Relations of trauma exposure with current religiousness and spirituality. *Mental Health, Religion & Culture*, *19*, 493–505.

Lipka, M., & Gecewicz, C. (September 6, 2017). *More Americans now say they're spiritual but not religious*. Pew Research Center. http://www.pewresearch.org/fact-tank/2017/09/06/more-americans-now-say-theyre-spiritual-but-not-religious.

Martin, C. G., Van Ryzin, M. J., & Dishion, T. J. (2016). Profiles of childhood trauma: Betrayal, frequency, and psychological distress in late adolescence. *Psychological Trauma: Theory, Research, Practice, and Policy*, *8*, 206–213.

Meyerson, D. A., Grant, K. E., Carter, J. S., & Kilmer, R. P. (2011). Posttraumatic growth among children and adolescents: A systematic review. *Clinical Psychology Review*, *31*, 949–964.

Pargament, K. I. (2002). The bitter and the sweet: An evaluation of the costs and benefits of religiousness. *Psychological Inquiry*, *13*, 168–181.

Pargament, K. I. (2006). The meaning of spiritual transformation. In J. D. Koss-Chiono, & P. Hefner (Eds.), *Spiritual transformation and healing: Anthropological, theological, neuroscientific, and clinical perspectives* (pp. 10–39). Walnut Creek, CA: AltaMira Press.

Pargament, K. I. (Ed.), (2013). *APA handbook of psychology, religion, and spirituality*. Washington, DC: American Psychological Association.

Pargament, K. I., Koenig, H. G., & Perez, L. M. (2000). The many methods of religious coping: Development and initial validation of the RCOPE. *Journal of Clinical Psychology*, *56*, 519–543.

Park, C. L., Currier, J. M., Harris, J. I., & Slattery, J. M. (2017). *Trauma, meaning, and spirituality: Translating research into clinical practice*. Washington, DC: American Psychological Association.

Pruyser, P. W. (1971). A psychological view of religion in the 1970s. *Bulletin of the Menninger Clinic*, *35*, 77–97.

ter Kuile, H., & Ehring, T. (2014). Predictors of changes in religiosity after trauma: Trauma, religiosity, and posttraumatic stress disorder. *Psychological Trauma: Theory, Research, Practice, and Policy*, *6*, 353–360.

Uwland-Sikkema, N. F., Visser, A., Westerhof, G. J., & Garssen, B. (2018). How is spirituality part of people's meaning system? *Psychology of Religion and Spirituality, 10*, 157–165.
Walker, D. F., Courtois, C. A., & Aten, J. D. (Eds.). (2015). *Spiritually oriented psychotherapy for trauma*. Washington, DC: American Psychological Association.
Wilt, J. A., Exline, J. J., Grubbs, J. B., Park, C. L., & Pargament, K. I. (2016). God's role in suffering: Theodicies, divine struggle, and mental health. *Psychology of Religion and Spirituality, 8*, 352–362.

Resources for clinicians and clients

Altmaier, E. M. (2017). *Push back the dark: Companioning adult survivors of childhood sexual abuse*. Eugene, OR: Wipf and Stock.
Bryant-Davis, T., & Wong, E. C. (2013). Faith to move mountains: Religious coping, spirituality, and interpersonal trauma recovery. *American Psychologist, 68*, 675–684.
Eriksson, C. B., & Yeh, D. (2012). Grounded transcendence: Resilience to trauma through spirituality and religion. In K. Gow, & M. J. Celinsky (Eds.), *Individual trauma: Recovering from deep wounds and exploring the potential for renewal* (pp. 53–71). Hauppauge, NY: Nova Science Publishers.
Finch, R. (2018). *A sparrow stirs its wings*. [Facebook online community Bruised But Not Broken]. https://suddendenouement.com.
Poulin, M. J., Silver, R. C., Gil-Rivas, V., Holman, E. A., & McIntosh, D. N. (2009). Finding social benefits after a collective trauma: Perceiving societal changes and well-being following 9/11. *Journal of Traumatic Stress, 22*, 81–90.
Treleaven, D. A. (2018). *Trauma-sensitive mindfulness: Practices for safe and transformative healing*. New York, NY: W.W. Norton and Company.
Walker, D. F., Courtois, C. A., & Aten, J. D. (Eds.). (2015). *Spiritually oriented psychotherapy for trauma*. Washington, DC: American Psychological Association.

Organization and integration of positive processes

9

Darin Strauss (2010) described his life divided into "before" and "after" in the wake of an automobile accident, in which he was the driver, that killed a high-school classmate. "For years, when I woke each morning, no matter where I was – home, my dorm, some friend's couch, a woman's bed – if I took an inventory of all that was good and bad in my life, the good would change (as it tends to do). But the bad remained a constant – Celine's unresolved death..." (p. 129). His account evokes many characteristics of trauma: immobilization, identity fixation, being "stuck" in the past, unable to gain from present experiences. He wrote a personal memoir of his life since the accident, a journey in which he achieved meaning, hope, and self-forgiveness, and concluded, "Things don't go away. They become you. There is no end, as T.S. Eliot somewhere says, but addition: the trailing consequence of further days and hours. No freedom from the past, or from the future. But we keep making our way, as we have to. We're all pretty much able to deal even with the worst that life can fire at us, if we simply admit that it is very difficult... We make our way, and effort and time give us cushion and dignity..." (pp. 202–203).

Anne Godlasky interviewed survivors of the Las Vegas mass shooting (https://www.usatoday.com/story/news/nation/2017/10/05/las-vegas-survivors-ptsd/726748001/). In her article, she noted after every mass shooting, about the time observers begin to feel compassion fatigue and care less about the shooting, survivors begin to go back to lives that existed before the trauma. But their re-engagement in life is challenging. Memories are triggered by obvious triggers (e.g., large crowds, loud noises) and by no triggers. Doubts and fears persist. Personal problems are made worse by friends who have "imagined deadlines" for when the survivor should be "over it." Recovery from trauma is a prolonged process for many who experience it. But the advice of Brandon Wolf, who survived the Pulse nightclub shooting in 2016, was as follows: "You are not alone. As much as you're going to want to feel alone and as easy as it will be to isolate yourself and wonder why not you – you're not alone."

These two quotes could be written by any survivor of trauma, events so violently damaging to our worldview that their occurrence divides life into "before" and "after." This text introduced positive psychology in the context of trauma, and identified six strengths researched by clinicians and researchers within the field of positive psychology that can serve as "positive processes" for trauma survivors. This concluding chapter considers how those strengths – hope, positive emotionality, resilience, forgiveness, meaning in life, and religiousness/spirituality – and others not discussed in this text penetrate barriers created by the trauma. The resources

Promoting Positive Processes after Trauma. DOI: https://doi.org/10.1016/B978-0-12-811975-4.00009-5
Copyright © 2019 Elsevier Inc. All rights reserved.

section lists a range of workbooks and texts that provide activities for use by clinician and client in identifying strengths, promoting them in meaningful ways against traumatic symptoms, and establishing a new secure base for life after trauma.

Trajectories after trauma

Impairment

As has been described in previous chapters, trajectories of life after trauma occur in relatively distinct ways: impairment, recovery, resilience, and growth. In terms of impairment, research documents that traumas of many kinds produce ongoing symptoms of arousal, cognitive distortions, coping failures, and escalating avoidance. Prospective studies of the development of post-traumatic stress disorder (PTSD) after trauma exist but are difficult to synthesize due to the wide variability in their measures of PTSD and limited types of participants (e.g., only combat survivors). Individual studies, however, clearly establish the presence of significant deterioration among trauma survivors. An early study (Shalev et al., 1998), for example, evaluated longitudinally the onset of PTSD and major depression among 200 trauma survivors recruited from the emergency room of a general hospital. In contrast to other studies of PTSD onset, the traumatic events were wide-ranging, encompassing traffic accidents, terrorist acts, physical assault, and domestic accidents. Follow-up interviews 1 and 4 months after baseline revealed that 30% of participants met criteria for PTSD at 1 month and 17%, at 4 months. Many individuals also met criteria for major depression: 19% at 1 month and 14% at 4 months.

Understanding the development of PTSD after a traumatic event might be biased by how research participants are identified. A recent study used a crowdsourcing website to compare responses regarding trauma trajectory to responses from traditionally recruited samples. Van Stolk-Cooke et al. (2018) obtained data on traumatic events, PTSD symptoms, depression, and anxiety from 1200 adults who volunteered through MTurk. Among 822 individuals reporting at least one event during their lifespan that met Criterion A for PTSD, the traumatic events included motor vehicle accidents, natural disasters, physical assault, and sexual assault. Prevalence of likely PTSD among this sample was 20%; for depression, 28%; and for anxiety, 22%.

Studies such as this and others might lead to the expectation that trauma results in functional impairment for a substantial minority of victims. However, researchers have documented wide variability in people's response to trauma. For example, Ozer, Best, Lipsey, and Weiss (2003) completed a *meta-analysis* of PTSD predictors. As part of that analysis, they noted the sharp contrast between the prevalence of lifetime exposure to a traumatic event (50–60%) and lifetime occurrence of PTSD (5–10%). If traumas do not inevitably lead to PTSD, what accounts for that variability?

Recovery

The Trauma Recovery Project (Holbrook, Anderson, Sieber, Browner, & Hoyt, 1998; Holbrook, Anderson, Sieber, Browner, & Hoyt, 1999) was a large scale epidemiological study examining outcomes after trauma. Over 1000 adults were followed for 12–18 months after their admission to a trauma center following events such as a motor vehicle accident, physical assault, and falls. Patients' reports on their quality of wellbeing (mobility, social activity, physical activity) revealed that a good recovery (score on well-being equal to 90% of pre-trauma wellbeing) was achieved by 60% of patients within the follow-up time period.

These data correspond to data from longitudinal studies, namely that people after trauma experience disequilibrium for a time (consider the 30% prevalence of PTSD in Shalev et al., 1998), but return to normal levels of physical and social functioning over an extended period. This positive conclusion is moderated by data suggesting that a resolution of the impairment trajectory is not universally present. For example, immediate depression and symptoms of PTSD among patients studied in the Trauma Recovery Project were strongly associated with later lower well-being, a finding that highlights the importance of focusing on psychosocial domains during recovery.

Resilience

Resilience is defined (see Southwick, Bonanno, Masten, Panter-Brick, & Yehuda, 2014) as a stable trajectory of functioning after an adverse event. Research has documented multiple determinants of resilience, including individual characteristics, cultural and social influences, and biological and genetic aspects. Yet unclear is how resilience is related to recovery. Does recovery signify that resilience was present? Does resilience improve recovery above what might be expected if the survivor had not had resilient qualities or resources?

Research has not adequately considered this question in part because of the difficulty in conducting longitudinal research that would adequately assess the constructs. Grolnick et al. (2018) argued that challenges to conducting research concerning adjustment and resilience among children experiencing disasters could be overcome by leveraging available data, partnering with communities to determine the most valuable data, and using nontraditional settings for program implementation.

Growth

Finally, research on post-traumatic growth reveals that after a wide range of traumatic events, many individuals display growth beyond what existed as personal characteristics before the trauma. Measures of post-traumatic growth (see Cann et al., 2010) categorize growth into five domains: improved interpersonal relationships, recognizing new possibilities for one's life, greater appreciation of life, greater sense of personal strengths, and spiritual transformation. A systematic review of post-traumatic growth among adults after interpersonal violence (Elderton, Berry, & Chan, 2017) revealed that post-traumatic growth occurred often (average 71%, range 58–99%) and usually within the appreciation of life domain.

Overall, we conclude that traumatic events happen frequently, and most adults and children experience one or more of them. After trauma, victims respond with apparent resilience; their function is unaffected and they do not show expected negative outcomes. Others show recovery; after initial struggles, their life returns to normal. Others respond with growth, where the trauma appears to have precipitated a struggle that resolves in improved mental health along observable dimensions. Others respond with impairment, manifesting symptoms that cause significant interference in daily living. It is clear that traumas are not uniform in their impact, nor are people uniform in their response to varying traumas. It is known that previous trauma experience exerts a deleterious impact on later trauma recovery. Promoting positive processes among clients seeking services after trauma therefore not only improves current function but also attenuates the influence of that trauma in future trauma experiences.

Positive processes and life after trauma

A recent model (Grych, Hamby, & Banyard, 2015; Hamby, Grych, & Banyard, 2018) suggests two amendments to descriptions in previous chapters of how positive processes improve life after trauma. Their model posits, first, that people have *portfolios* of strengths: more of some and less of others on any given occasion, as well as more or fewer strengths overall. When individuals thrive after trauma, they are revealing a portfolio with many strengths (*poly-strengths*), or with strengths of greater influence (*signature strengths*). Yet unknown is whether poly-strengths, a term the model developers use for having a large number of strengths, is more important to recovery than strengths which directly correspond to the needs posed by the trauma or strengths that are more successful for the person in general. For example, after a natural disaster, having signature strengths of an interpersonal nature such as compassion and generativity would allow the victim to access help from strangers and to reach out in empathy to other victims.

What are signature strengths? Peterson and Seligman (2004) presented the idea of signature strengths, numbering between 3 to 7 out of the 24, which best characterize each person. Taking an inventory of strengths and using the top ranked strengths is the most direct means of identifying signature strengths, but that would not be a parsimonious or valid measure during post-trauma life. Some analyses of strengths (e.g., Peterson, 2006) contemplated two dimensions along which an individual could place himself or herself: strengths of the mind versus the heart, and strengths that are self-directed versus other-directed. Alternately, an interview such as that used by Cheavens, Strunk, Lazarus, and Goldstein (2012) could assist in clients identifying signature strengths by defining four domains (cognitive, interpersonal, behavioral, and acceptance) and querying whether participants used strategies or approaches from that domain and with what success.

The second amendment suggested by the model is that strengths succeed within pathways – mechanisms or routes – by which strengths improve function after trauma. The first is the *pathway of regulation*, the pathway of dealing with the threats of trauma. Examples of those threats are intrusive thoughts and memories, unwanted flashbacks, debilitating arousal, immobilization in the face of fear – all threats that feel like an attack from outside. Managing distressing emotions is an outcome of regulation, allowing negative emotions to exist and be recognized while not being overwhelmed by them. Using emotions to stimulate the broaden-and-build sequence is important to regulation as well. Having resilience is relevant to regulation, employing persistence and hardiness to ground one's efforts. Hope is an essential element of regulation, particularly using role models to establish goals and pathways to recovery.

The second is the *pathway of meaning-making*. Meaning-making pathways are present when strengths promote a transformative perspective. This perspective operates against the phenomenon of being trapped inside after trauma, detached from all others, suffering harm to one's identity, feeling weak and depressed. Religiousness and spirituality and meaning in life are transformative strengths. One's orientation toward optimism is relevant to the meaning-making pathway, more optimism promoting self-acceptance and purpose in life. The collective experience of trauma, feeling connected to humanity as opposed to the isolated experience, is also critical to meaning making since it rests on common shared adversity.

The third is the *pathway of interpersonal interactions*. Through this pathway operate strengths that enable victims to approach others for support, such as hope, forgiveness, and humility, and to allow others in turn to provide care and resources back to victims. Interpersonal interactions additionally establish the ground for accurate narratives about the trauma experience, allowing feedback to the victim to correct inaccurate observations and increase perceptions of resources available to counter the traumatic struggles. The generativity often stimulated by the trauma experience that shows itself in a better understanding of others' similar experiences relies on greater empathy that is a strength following the pathway of interpersonal interaction.

In an extensive study of over 2000 adults and adolescents from a low-income community, Hamby et al. (2018) investigated three outcomes after trauma: subjective well-being, post-traumatic growth, and mental health. The traumatic events experienced by the participants varied widely, and included relational aggressions (betrayal, bullying), physical assault, parental neglect, and exposure to violence. Further, the sample had typically experienced more than one trauma: 32% reported 2 and 59%, 3. The authors composed outcome variables reflecting a concept they termed "thriving": in order to be considered thriving, the scores on the outcome measures needed to be at least 0.5 standard deviations above the mean. The three groups of outcome variables were subjective well-being (e.g., life satisfaction), post-traumatic growth (a post-traumatic growth inventory), and mental health (e.g., depression).

Their results supported previously noted findings, and established new findings. First, thriving in terms of subjective well-being was influenced by strengths within all pathways: the regulatory pathway strength of persistence, meaning making pathway strength of hope, and interpersonal pathway strength of generativity (love and kindness). Post-traumatic growth thriving was associated with strengths within all pathways: the regulatory pathway strengths of persistence and emotional expression; the meaning-making strengths of purpose and religiousness; and the interpersonal strength of compassion. Mental health thriving was predicted by strengths in two pathways: regulatory pathway strength of emotional awareness and expression, and meaning-making strength of hope.

In summary, this research has suggested both importance and organization among strengths. First, the most important strengths for this large sample in dealing with many types and instances of adversity were endurance (bravery and persistence), emotional awareness, purpose (wisdom), generativity (love and kindness), and compassion. Additionally, for all participants, having multiple strengths, termed polystrengths, was uniquely and positively associated with all outcomes. Second, the statistical analyses revealed that strengths predicted outcomes over and above what was accounted for by demographics and characteristics of adversity. Third, purpose was related to outcomes across all three thriving measures, underlying its importance.

The portfolio approach to thinking about personal strengths has implications for clinicians in how to foster the use of strengths after trauma. First, it suggests the importance of *increased self-knowledge*: knowledge of one's personal strengths and especially signature strengths. Since impairment in living caused by trauma influences low estimation of personal resources, it is a key first step for clients to be aware of their personal strengths. For example, an intervention for homeless young adults (Krabbenborg et al., 2015) focused on identifying personal strengths resulted in improved quality of life on several measures and also continuance in receiving care.

A related question in helping clients identify and promote personal strengths poses an interesting dilemma. When using strengths to help with recovery, is it better to rely on signature strengths, a *capitalization model*, or to focus on remediating deficiencies in strengths, a *compensation model*? Research in an adjacent area of application, personal growth interventions, conducted by Meyers, van Woerkom, de Reuver, Bakk, and Oberski (2015) directly compared these models among young adults. A treatment composed to operationalize the capitalization model (identify one's signature strengths and learn to use them in new ways) resulted in increased resilience and hope compared to a treatment operationalizing the compensation model (identify strengths where one was deficit and increase them). Similar findings were noted in a psychotherapy study of depression (Cheavens et al., 2012) where treatment using a capitalization model achieved faster and better outcomes than a treatment focusing on relative deficits.

A second implication for the clinician is to help clients view their signature strengths as *applicable across the domains* of trauma symptoms. Hope, for example, might counter being attacked from outside by establishing goals and determining pathways for achieving them, emphasizing a strong sense of efficacy. Being trapped inside could respond to increased hope with a transformative view, using meaning-making and religiousness/spirituality to foster more positive emotions and creating interest and curiosity. Last, a distorted view of self and situation may be affected positively by hope in establishing compassion and generativity.

A third implication for promoting positive processes is to understand that trauma not only creates opportunity for growth but essentially is *required for growth.* Janoff-Bulman (2004) outlined three ways in which she believes that position is supported by research on adversity. First, research indicates that, in a manner similar to where pushing oneself physically creates physical strength, challenging oneself psychologically creates similar psychological strength. Post-traumatic growth research frequently reports that survivors become aware of personal strengths and resources and also develop new skills and resources under adverse conditions. "Survivors learn about themselves – their competencies, abilities, and new possibilities – in the course of expending tremendous effort and determination during their post trauma adjustment, and they see themselves differently at the end of this painstaking process" (Janoff-Bulman, 2004, p. 31). Second, adversity creates psychological preparedness for subsequent adversities in life. As examples, new identities are created and new global beliefs are constructed. Third, trauma promotes the existential reevaluation of one's world, including one's own values and their match or mismatch with tasks of living. This reevaluation may include new emphases on interpersonal attachment, new priorities in life, and spiritual transformations.

A last implication is that clinicians have multiple methods, adjunctive to therapy goals, by which to promote positive processes. There are published workbooks with exercises to promote goals such as finding meaning, establishing new priorities, and beginning advocacy for others. Within the resources section at the conclusion of this chapter are many examples of those publications. Additionally, there are many digital resources available. The Positive Psychology Center at the University of Pennsylvania (ppc.sas.upenn.edu) offers an array of resources, books, links, readings, and videos. Promoting positive processes can be a goal of treatment, or a means for integration of treatment goals.

Summary

Well-being after trauma is a task that Van der Kolk termed "self-leadership" (2014). The client must first get to know the "internal landscape," requiring self-compassion over and above all else. The stories of the trauma must be revisited, creating new narratives and filling in gaps. Creating new possibilities rests on hope and resilience. Reducing avoidance requires forgiveness and empathy. Religiousness and spirituality may allow a new frame for the understanding of the trauma and new outlines for the journey ahead. The components of flourishing are steps along that journey: self-acceptance, openness to new experience, purpose in life, relationships with others, personal autonomy, and environmental mastery.

References

Cann, A., Calhoun, L. G., Tedeschi, R. G., Taku, K., Vishnevsky, T., Triplett, K. N., & Danhauer, S. C. (2010). A short form of the posttraumatic growth inventory. *Anxiety, Stress & Coping: An International Journal*, *23*, 127–137.

Cheavens, J. S., Strunk, D. R., Lazarus, S. A., & Goldstein, L. A. (2012). The compensation and capitalization models: A test of two approaches to individualizing the treatment of depression. *Behaviour Research and Therapy*, *50*, 699–706.

Elderton, A., Berry, A., & Chan, C. (2017). A systematic review of posttraumatic growth in survivors of interpersonal violence in adulthood. *Trauma, Violence, & Abuse*, *18*, 223–236.

Grolnick, W. S., Schonfeld, D. J., Schreiber, M., Cohen, J., Cole, V., Jaycox, L., . . . Zatzick, D. (2018). Improving adjustment and resilience in children following a disaster: Addressing research challenges. *American Psychologist*, *73*, 215–229.

Grych, J., Hamby, S., & Banyard, V. (2015). The resilience portfolio model: Understanding healthy adaptation in victims of violence. *Psychology of Violence*, *5*, 343–354.

Hamby, S., Grych, J., & Banyard, V. (2018). Resilience portfolios and poly-strengths: Identifying protective factors associated with thriving after adversity. *Psychology of Violence*, *8*, 172–183.

Holbrook, T. L., Anderson, J. P., Sieber, W. J., Browner, D., & Hoyt, D. B. (1998). Outcome after major trauma: Discharge and 6 month follow-up results from the Trauma Recovery Project. *Journal of Traumatology*, *45*, 315–323, 1998.

Holbrook, T. L., Anderson, J. P., Sieber, W. J., Browner, D., & Hoyt, D. B. (1999). Outcome after major trauma: 12-month and 18-month follow-up results from the Trauma Recovery Project. *Journal of Traumatology*, *46*, 765–771, 1999.

Janoff-Bulman, R. (2004). Posttraumatic growth: Three explanatory models. *Psychological Inquiry*, *15*, 30–34.

Krabbenborg, M. A. M., Boersma, S. N., van der Veld, W. M., van Hulst, B., Vollebergh, W. A. M., & Wolf, J. R. L. M. (2015). A cluster randomized controlled trial testing the effectiveness of Houvast: A strengths-based intervention for homeless young adults. *Research on Social Work Practice*. Available from https://doi.org/10.1177/1049731515622263.

Meyers, M. C., van Woerkom, M., de Reuver, R. S. M., Bakk, Z., & Oberski, D. L. (2015). Enhancing psychological capital and personal growth initiative: Working on strengths or deficiencies. *Journal of Counseling Psychology*, *62*, 50–62.

Ozer, E. J., Best, S. R., Lipsey, T. L., & Weiss, D. S. (2003). Predictors of posttraumatic stress disorder and symptoms in adults: A meta-analysis. *Psychological Bulletin*, *129*, 52–73.

Peterson, C. (2006). *A primer in positive psychology*. New York, NY: Oxford University Press.

Peterson, C., & Seligman, M. E. P. (2004). *Character strengths and virtues: A handbook and classification*. Washington, DC: American Psychological Association and New York, NY: Oxford University Press.

Shalev, A. Y. I., Freedman, S., Peri, T., Brandes, D., Sahar, T., Orr, S., & Pitman, R. K. (1998). Prospective study of posttraumatic stress disorder and depression following trauma. *American Journal of Psychiatry*, *155*, 630–637.

Southwick, S. M., Bonanno, G. A., Masten, A. S., Panter-Brick, C., & Yehuda, R. (2014). Resilience definitions, theory, and challenges: Interdisciplinary perspectives. *European Journal of Psychotraumatology*, *5*. Available from https://doi.org/10.3402/ejpt.v5.25338.

Van der Kolk, B. (2014). *The body keeps the score: Brain, mind, and body in the healing of trauma*. New York, NY: Viking Press.

Van Stolk-Cooke, K., Brown, A., Maheux, A., Parent, J., Forehand, R., & Price, M. (2018). Crowdsourcing trauma: Psychopathology in a trauma-exposed sample recruited via mechanical Turk. *Journal of Traumatic Stress*. Available from https://doi.org/10.1002/jts.22303.

Resources for clinicians and clients

Ambler, G., Anstey, M. P., McCall, T. D., & White, M. A. (2017). *Flourishing in faith: Theology encountering positive psychology*. Eugene, OR: Wipf and Stock Publishers.

Chang, E. C., Downey, C. A., Hirsch, J. K., & Lin, N. J. (2016). *Positive psychology in racial and ethnic groups*. Washington, DC: American Psychological Association.

Copeland, M. E., & Harris, M. (2000). *Healing the trauma of abuse: A women's workbook*. Oakland, CA: New Harbinger Publications.

Curran, L. (2010). *Trauma competency: A clinician's guide*. Eau Claire, WI: PESI Publications.

Follette, V., & Pistorello, J. (2007). *Finding life beyond trauma*. Oakland, CA: New Harbinger Publications.

Joseph, S. (Ed.). (2015). *Positive psychology in practice: Promoting human flourishing in work, health, education, and everyday life* (2nd ed.). Hoboken, NJ: John Wiley & Sons.

Leutenberg, E. R. A., & Liptak, J. J. (2015). *Managing trauma workbook: A toolbox of reproducible assessments and activities for facilitators*. Duluth, MN: Whole Person Stress and Wellness Publishers.

Lopez, S. J., Pedrotti, J. T., & Snyder, C. R. (2015). *Positive psychology: The scientific and practical explorations of human strengths* (3rd ed.). New York, NY: Sage.

Proctor, C. (Ed.). (2017). *Positive psychology interventions in practice*. New York, NY: Springer.

Schiraldi, G. R. (2017). *The resilience workbook: Essential skills to recover from stress, trauma, and adversity*. Oakland, CA: New Harbinger Publications.

Schwartz, A. (2017). *The complex PTSD workbook: A mind-body approach to regaining emotional control & becoming whole*. Berkeley, CA: Althea Press.

Strauss, D. (2010). *Half a life*. New York, NY: Random House.

Tedeschi, R. G., & Moore, B. A. (2016). *The posttraumatic growth workbook*. Oakland, CA: New Harbinger Publications.

Treleaven, D. A. (2018). *Trauma-sensitive mindfulness: Practices for safe and transformative healing*. New York, NY: W.W. Norton & Company.

Glossary of terms

Accommodation Cognitive processes undertaken to change global beliefs after they are disconfirmed by events such as traumas; an example would be to discard the belief that we receive what we deserve [justice] and adopt the new belief that life will not always treat us fairly.

Adverse Childhood Experiences (ACE) The term used to denote a range of events and influences during childhood that involve neglect, abuse, familial and community violence, and abandonment.

Affect A general and accessible state of being. Examples are pleasure, fatigue, displeasure, and vigor.

Assets Characteristics of a family or social environment that increase positive outcomes and well-being among all members of the environment.

Assimilation Cognitive processes undertaken to change situational meanings when they are in conflict with global beliefs; an example would be to redefine an event from being uncontrollable to one where some control can be exerted over personal outcomes even if the event was not avoided.

Avoidance coping Ways of dealing with traumatic events that emphasize avoidance of situations and feelings, including denial, distortion, and withdrawal.

Betrayal trauma Interpersonal trauma inflicted by a person trusted by the victim, in a context where the victim is dependent on the offender, and where victim and offender are in an ongoing relationship; examples are family, church, military, and sports teams.

Broaden-and-build theory A model for how positive emotions create a transformation. A person experiences positive emotions and is encouraged to expand thought–action links. Following those new links to action creates capacity (physical, social, intellectual) and increases positive emotions. Those emotions further stimulate new thought–action links, eventually resulting in an upward spiral.

Bullying Frequent, systematic peer-to-peer interpersonal, psychological, and physical harassment and aggression.

Capitalization model Relying on strengths typically and successfully used in adversity in the past, and using those strengths in a new way.

Chronic embitterment After an offense, the victim experiences in an ongoing way the extremes of anger and bitterness, believes these extremes are justified by the offense, and ruminates over the offense and its impact.

Compensation model Identifying deficit strengths and attempting to increase their use and effectiveness in adversity.

Condoning Minimizing the offense committed by a perpetrator against a victim by reducing its impact and defining the action as acceptable.

Cumulative risk The additive effects of simultaneous or sequential risk factors; the accretion over time of challenges of adversity.

Disease model A way of understanding symptoms or problems where the sole origin is presumed to be inside a person (traits, behaviors) rather than caused by interaction of person and environment. A disease model would diagnose the pathology and devise treatment to remove it.

Emotion The combination of arousal, an appraisal, and behavioral expression. Examples are fear and anger.

Emotional approach Moving toward rather than away from emotions, including distressing emotions. Emotional approach consists of emotional processing (active attempts to explore and understand emotions) and emotional expression.

Emotional schemas Personal models of emotions in general. Examples are "emotions are bad and I should avoid them" or "expressing all emotions is better than keeping them locked up."

Epigenetic inheritance The influence of environmental factors on gene expression that are passed on to offspring. May be a route by which extreme adversity among parents creates stress reactions among children.

Flourishing Fully realizing one's own potential in areas of self-acceptance, personal growth, purpose in life, relationships with others, mastery over the environment, and autonomous living.

Hardiness The quality of having strength, toughness, stamina, and persistence over time in spite of events that are adverse or traumatic.

Hygiology Study of aspects of personality and character that influence a person's effectiveness in life under both favorable and adverse circumstances.

Life review A structured interview-based treatment centered on one or more themes (e.g., work, life turning points, death, and dying) that prompts participants to develop narratives, using the process of narrative development and revision to increase valuing of past events and their connections to the present.

Meaning in life A perspective on life that emphasizes the purpose and connection of experienced events to the future or the past, the inherent value of those events, the continuity of connections across periods of time, and the coherence of connections among types of events.

Meaning-making Any effort to reduce the emotional distress that occurs when events are highly discrepant with the individual's history of beliefs and assumptions about the world, himself or herself, and the interactions over time between self and world.

Meta-analysis A way of conducting research where published studies conforming to pre-established criteria are statistically analyzed to reveal overall findings across multiple data sets.

Mood A diffuse and broad state of mind or feeling not linked in time with any particular cause.

Mobbing Bullying occurring in work settings among adults that leads to spiraling personal and corporate damage including absenteeism and organizational culture.

Moral injury A source of stress during combat where service members are required to participate in, witness, or overlook actions that violate their own moral code. Common reactions are shame, depression, and rumination.

Negative hedonic beliefs The belief that happiness cannot occur in the presence of physical, mental, or social painful circumstances.

Optimism Believing that successful outcomes are going to occur in the future in spite of any adversity.

Pathology Focus on probable or likely causes of disease or condition after establishing its presence.

Pathway of interpersonal interactions A route of influence of personal strengths that enable victims of trauma to approach others for instrumental help and emotional support and, in turn, to provide care and support to others.

Pathway of meaning-making A route of influence of personal strengths that enable trauma survivors to acquire a transformative perspective, where difficulties are seen in a new way that enables additional recovery and growth.

Pathway of regulation A route of influence where personal strengths are used by the trauma victim to deal effectively with aspects of trauma that create dislocation: increased arousal, fear, detachment, weakness and fatigue, and withdrawal and isolation.

PERMA A model of happiness that incorporates positive emotions, engagement, interpersonal relationships, meaning, and accomplishments.

Persistence Not avoiding or backing away from threats, challenges, difficulties, or painful circumstances over time.

Personal theories A way of understanding people's response to events through how their own lens, or perception, organizes how they see and interpret events. This lens may not be explicit or even recognized by the person.

Placebo A substance that is presumably inert or not active; used in research comparing a treatment to a plausible placebo in which the participant has faith in its success.

Portfolio The density and diversity of resources available to a survivor that shape their response to the trauma.

Poly-strengths Within a portfolio of resources, having a larger number of strengths and protective factors.

Positivity Prioritizing experiences that lead to positive emotions rather than pursuing happiness.

Post-traumatic growth Enduring positive changes after the experience of trauma that occur in distinct life domains: interpersonal relationships, future directions, appreciation of life, awareness of personal strengths, religiousness/spirituality.

Protective factors Variables connected with a positive outcome after adversity that are characteristics of the victim (e.g., problem-solving skills) or of the social and physical environment (e.g., close family relationships, community organizations).

Reconciliation A process that occurs over time and involves both the victim and the offender, where the offender acknowledges guilt and remorse and seeks to restore the former relationship with the victim.

Recovery A change for the better in a set of circumstances in which symptoms of illness were present but no longer are present or, if so, no longer challenge psychological or physical health.

Religiousness Holding personal beliefs about God or a deity that create a framework of meaning, that encourage participation in individual and group religious activities and rituals, that motivate adherence to moral codes of behaviors, and that provide a sense of identification with a community of like-minded individuals.

Risk Circumstances that create a likelihood of a negative outcome, whether physically challenging (e.g., violence), emotionally challenging (e.g., abuse), or socially challenging (e.g., poverty).

Resilience Positive adaptation during or after significant adversity or risk for adversity; responding with adaptation rather than impairment to circumstances that challenge physical and mental health.

Self-compassion Staying open to one's own suffering, failures, and setbacks while avoiding judgmental views of oneself; viewing oneself kindly, as part of common humanity, and with a balanced awareness of thoughts and feelings.

Shell shock Term used during World War I to describe soldiers' injuries, which included psychological and physical damage, thought to occur from proximity to exploding shells rather than direct wounding.

Signature strengths Character strengths, numbering from 3 to 7, that especially depict a person's resources and responses, strengths typically used with success in circumstances ranging from difficult to traumatic.

Spirituality Ongoing personal experience of a deep connection to the sacred or divine, including personal activities that increase this connection, behaviors and beliefs that relate to goals of ultimate significance, and a mindful balanced emphasis on inner and outer lives.

Spiritual transformation A fundamental change in the importance of spirituality in the life of an individual. Positive spiritual transformation is the most frequent association with the term "transformation," which is an acceleration in the value of spiritual experiences, frameworks, and priorities. Spiritual transformation can be also negative, which is a reduction in the personal value assigned to spirituality.

Strengths Positive traits that are owned by a person and frequently applied in everyday life. Examples are creativity, the trait of thinking of novel ways to view life and to solve problems, and modesty, the trait of avoiding the promotion of oneself and one's successes.

Subjective well-being The hedonic definition of a good life, that happiness occurs when one has high levels of positive emotions, low levels of negative emotions, and high levels of life satisfaction.

Trauma-informed Designing human services to take into account potential trauma histories among users; examples are community health services that emphasize safety, empowerment, and choice for clients in areas such as treatment decision making.

Traumatic stressors External events that create trauma that may not be personally experienced, may not involve physical injury, or may not appear likely to lead to impairment; examples are hearing about a close relative's violent death and workplace bullying.

Virtues A set of strengths valued across cultures and time periods for their contribution to personal and societal success. Examples are humanity and courage.

Index

A

Accommodations, 81
ACE. *See* Adverse Childhood Experiences (ACE)
Achterhof, R., 26
Adams, K., 9
Adult mortality, 17–18
Adverse Childhood Experiences (ACE), 55
Adversity, 107
Affect, 43. *See also* Emotions
Affect regulation, 7–8
Afghanistan, war in, 10–11
Agency, 33
Akhtar, S., 69
Allemand, M., 69
Altmaier, E. M., 65, 82
Alzheimer's disease, 17
Anxiety, 17
Armed conflict, 11
Armstrong, D., 4, 9
Arousal regulation, 7–8
Arousal symptoms, 6
Assets, 56
Assimilations, 81
Autonomy, 19. *See also* Subjective well-being
Avoidance coping, 44

B

Bacevice, P. A., 23–24
Barker, C., 9
Barker, M., 3
Barlow, J., 69
Barnes, J. E., 9
Barton, Y. A., 96
Baumeister, R. F., 78–80, 84
Bell, A., 10
Benefit finding, 25
Bereavement, 4
Bernstein, R. E., 10
Bertold, A., 34
Best, S. R., 102
Betrayal trauma, 9–10
Bhushan, B., 95
Bierer, L.M., 10
Bird, V., 36
Birrell, P. J., 10
Bliss, D., 79
Boals, A., 84
Boals, A., 5
Boehm, J. K., 21
Bonanno, G. A., 24, 57–58
Boston Marathon bombings, 2
Boynston, H. M., 93
Branch, S., 3
Broaden-and-build theory of positive emotions, 45
Brown, B., 38
Bryant-Davis, T., 95
Buddhist, 95
Bullying, 3. *See also* Peer-to-peer violence
Burman, M., 66

C

Cambodian community leaders, 26
Cannon, W. B., 6
Capitalization model, 106
Carter, J. S., 95
Case, A., 17–18
Center for Positive Organizations at University of Michigan, 23
Centers for Disease Control, 4, 55
Charney, D. S., 61
Charry, E. T., 23
Cheadle, A. C. D., 69
Cheung, F. M., 79
Cheung, M. W. L., 5
Cheung, S. F., 79
Child sexual abuse, 9
Christian, 95

Christopher, J. S., 22
Ciarrocchi, J. W., 34
Cognitions, alterations in, 6
Cognitive process, hope as, 32–33
Combat in trauma, 10–11. *See also* Military trauma
Common humanity, 21
Communal scale, 26
Community, 23–24
Compassion fatigue, 9. *See also* Vicarious trauma
Compensation model, 106
Condoning, 67
Conroy, A., 69–70
Cook, R., 11–12
Coping
avoidance, 44
meaning-focused, 44
Cornish, M. A., 69–70
Courage, 20. *See also* Subjective well-being
Coworking, 23–24
Crespo, M., 6–7
Culturally embedded strengths, 22
Cultures, positive psychology and, 22
Cumulative risk, 56
Currier, J. M., 59–60

D
Daring Greatly (Brown), 38
da Silva, A. B., 66
Davis, C. G., 82
Deaton, A., 17–18
de Bohlmeijer, E. T., 21–22
Defense Department of the United States, 3
Dementia, 17
Deneke, E., 34
Depression, 17
Despair, 31. *See also* Hope
Diagnostic and Statistical Manual, 2
Diener, E., 18
Disease model, 17
Dishion, T. J., 93
Distortion of reality, 8
DMS-5, 9
Duckworth, A. L., 18
Dy-Liacco, G. S., 34

E
Eaves, E. R., 32
Ehring, T., 92
Einarsen, S., 3
Eliot, T. S., 101
Embodied process, hope as, 34–35
Emotional disorders, 17
Emotionality, 43
Emotions, 43
classification scheme, 43
defined, 43
negative. *See* Negative emotions
positive. *See* Positive emotions
Endurance, 106
Enright, R. D., 67
Environmental disasters, 4
Environmental mastery, subjective well-being and, 19
Eudaimonic models, 18
Evans, W. R., 92
Existential process, hope as, 33

F
Facebook, 3
Faith-driven hope, 33–34
Fear, N. T., 2
Fehr, R., 67–68
Fernandez-Lansac, V., 6–7
Fitzgibbons, R. P., 67
Flourishing, 18
work-related, 23
Folkman, S., 8
Forgiveness
after trauma, 69–71
defined/defining, 66–69
overview, 65–66
promoting, 71–73
questions, 66
Fowler, D. R., 33
Frankl, V. E., 77
Freezing. *See* Immobilization
Freire, K. E., 4
Freyd, J. J., 10
Fridlund, B., 66

G
Gallup News poll, 23
Garcia, C., 82
Garrett, L. E., 23–24
Gelfand, M. J., 67–68
Generativity, 106
George, L. S., 94–95
Global goals, 81–82

Glover, N., 9
Goals, 32
God, 81–82
Godlasky, Anne, 101
Grant, K. E., 95
Guldbrand, M., 66

H

Hale, A. E., 92–93
Hamm, A. O., 6
Happiness. *See also* Subjective well-being
  defined, 43
Hardiness, 57–58
Harper, A. R., 95
Harris, J. I., 59–60
Harris, K. A., 90
Heffernan, M. E., 69
Heintzelman, S. J., 84
Held, P., 11
Herman, J., 1, 35–36
Hickinbottom, S., 22
Hill, P. L., 69
Ho, M. Y., 79
Holas, P., 72
Holocaust survivors, 10
Hooker, S. A., 79
Hope, 20
  after trauma, 35–37
  characteristics, 31
  as cognitive process, 32–33
  defined, 31–35
  as embodied process, 34–35
  as existential process, 33
  as faith-driven process, 33–34
  overview, 31–32
  promoting, 37–39
  scientific study, 31
Hopeful people, 31
Howell, D. S., 90
Humanity, 20
Hussain, D., 95
Huta, V., 19–20
Hygiology, 17

I

Iacoviello, B. M., 61
Identity, trauma effects on, 8
Immigration, 11–12
Immobilization, 7
Impairment, 24, 102
Intergenerational trauma transmission, 10. *See also* Transgenerational transmission
Interpersonal interactions, pathway of, 105
Interpersonal relationships. *See also* Subjective well-being
  post-traumatic growth, 26
  subjective well-being, 22
Interventions, positive psychology, 25
Intimate partner violence, 4
In-transit traumas, 11–12
Intrusive symptoms, 6
Iraq, war in, 10–11
Irritable mood, 43

J

James, William, 89
Janoff-Bulman, R., 5, 25–26, 80–81
Jayawickreme, E., 79
Jeste, D. V., 57
Jones, E., 2
Justice, 20. *See also* Subjective well-being

K

Kashdan, T. B., 77
Kennedy, M.C., 25–26
Keyes, C. L. M., 18
Khmer Rouge genocide, 26
Kilmer, R. P., 95
King, L.A., 84
Klappa, S. P., 33
Kleine, E., 21–22
Kong, L., 59
Kosits, R. D., 23
Krakauer, M., 24
Krejtz, I., 72

L

Laboratory studies, 6
Landau, M. J., 78–80, 84
Las Vegas mass shooting, 101
Lazarus, R. S., 8
Leamy, M., 36
Le Boutillier, C., 36
Lee, S. Y., 92–93
Lehman, D. R., 82
Leontiev, D., 22
Letts, J., 11–12

Levi, O., 37
Li, T., 25
Liechtentritt, R., 37
Life
meaning in. *See* Meaning
philosophy of, 24
purpose in, 19
Life after trauma
forgiveness, 69–71
hope, 35–37
meaning, 80–83
positive processes, 104–107
recovery, 24, 103
religiousness and spirituality, 92–94
resilience, 24, 59–60, 103
trajectories of. *See* Trajectories of life after trauma
Life review, 84
Life satisfaction, 43
Lindy, J. D., 77
Linley, P. A., 22
Lipsey, T. L., 102
Lopez, S. J., 21, 37–38, 56, 65
Lorentz, D., 77
Low, A., 6
Ludwig, T. E., 69
Luna, L. R., 70
Lyubomirsky, S., 21

M

Maddux, L., 9
Malone, M. R., 79
Man's Search for Meaning (Frankl), 77
Marjory Stoneman Douglas High School shootings, 95
Martin, C. G., 93
Mass shooting, Las Vegas, 101
Mass violence, 2–3
Masten, A. S., 59
Masters, K. S., 79
Matthiesen, S., 3
McAdams, D. P., 60–61
McMahan, E. A., 20
Meaning
after trauma, 80–83
defined/defining, 78–80
overview, 77–78
promoting, 84–85
questions, 78
Meaning-focused coping, 44
Meaning-making, 81, 89
pathways, 105
Memories, 101
Mental health
refugees, 11–12
thriving, 105–106
Mercy, J. A., 4
Merrell, K. W., 60
Meta-analysis, 33
Meyerson, D. A., 95
Migration, 11–12
Military trauma, 10–11
Miller, L., 96
Miller, S. A., 33
Mindfulness, 21
Miron, L. R., 21–22
Mobbing, 3
Mood, 43. *See also* Emotions
Mood, alterations in, 6
Moore, B. A., 7–8
Moral code, 11
Moral injury, 11
Morgan, M. S., 82
Morris, G., 69–70
Motor vehicle accidents, 5
Multidimensional Existential Meaning Scale, 79
Mysticism, 95

N

Nag, M., 67–68
National Red Cross, 4
Natural disasters, 4
Nazi concentration camps, 10
Neff, K., 21
Negative emotions, 44–45
Negative goals, 32
Nes, L. S., 33
Neurocognitive disorders, 17
Nezlek, J. B., 72
Noll, J. G., 9

O

Offspring of Holocaust Survivors (OHS), 10
Okubo, Y., 26
Optimism, 33. *See also* Hope
Orcutt, H. K., 21–22
Organizational behavior, 23
Ozer, E. J., 102

P
Pargament, K. I., 95
Park, C. L., 25–26, 59–60, 79–81, 92–95
Park, N., 20
Pathology, 17
Pathways, 32
  interpersonal interactions, 105
  meaning-making, 105
  regulation, 105
Pedrotti, J. T., 56, 65
Peer-to-peer violence, 3
People, trauma effects on, 6–8
  arousal and affect regulation, 7–8
  distortion of reality, 8
  identity, 8
  immobilization/freezing, 7
PERMA, 19
Persistence, 57–58
Persistent Complex Bereavement Disorder, 4
Personal growth, 19. *See also* Subjective well-being
Personal theories, 36
Peterson, C., 20
Peterson, S. J., 69
Philosophy of life, 25
Placebo, 34
Poly-strengths, 104
Portfolios of strengths, 104
Positive emotionality, promoting, 49–50
Positive emotions
  avoidance coping, 44
  broaden-and-build theory, 45
  meaning-focused coping, 44
  personal narrative on deficit of, 46–47
  role of, 44–47
Positive goals, 32
Positive organizations, 23. *See also* Organizational behavior
Positive psychology
  cultures and, 22
  description, 18
  forgiveness. *See* Forgiveness
  hope. *See* Hope
  interventions, 24
  meaning. *See* Meaning
  organizational behavior, 23
  religion and, 23
  religiousness. *See* Religiousness
  self-compassion, 21
  spirituality. *See* Spirituality
  subjective well-being. *See* Subjective well-being
Positive Psychology Center at the University of Pennsylvania, 107
Positive role of all emotions, 47–49
Post-traumatic growth, 81, 103–104
  interpersonal relationships, 25
  measures of, 103–104
  philosophy of life, 25
  research in, 26–27
  sense of self, 25
  thriving, 105–106
Post-traumatic self, 47
Post-traumatic stress disorder (PTSD), 2. *See also* Positive psychology; Trauma
  memories, 6–7
  symptoms, 6
Promotion
  forgiveness, 71–73
  hope, 37–39
  meaning, 84–85
  religiousness and spirituality, 94–97
  resilience, 60–62
Protective factors, 56
Psychological Trauma: Theory, Research, Practice, and Policy, 70
Psychology
  hygiology, 17
  pathology, 17
Psychology of Religion and Spirituality (Schnitker & Emmons), 23
Purpose in life, 19
Putnam, F. W., 9

R
Ramsay, S., 3
Reality, distortion of, 8
Reconciliation, 67
Recovery
  hope and, 36–37
  tasks involved in, 36
  trajectories of life after trauma, 24, 103
Refugees. *See* Immigration
Regulation, pathway of, 105
Relationships. *See* Interpersonal relationships

Religion, 23
Religiousness. *See also* Spirituality
after trauma, 92–94
defined/defining, 89–91
overview, 89–90
positive and negative influences, 96
promoting, 94–97
questions, 90
Resilience
defined/defining, 56–58
life after trauma, 24, 59–60, 103
overview, 55–56
promoting, 60–62
questions, 56
Riffle, O. M., 79
Risk, 56
cumulative, 56
Roepke, A. M., 79
Rosen, R. I., 79
Roxberg, A., 66
Ruch, W., 34
Rusanowska, M., 72
Ryan, R. M., 19–20
Ryff, C. D., 18, 79
Ryff's model, 18

S
Savaya, R., 37
Scherer, M., 69
Schizophrenia, 17
Schmeidler, J., 10
School shootings, 2–3
Schuler, E. R., 5
Schultz, J. M., 65
Seawall, A. H., 69
Secondary traumatic stress. *See* Vicarious trauma
Segerstrom, S. C., 33
Self, sense of, 25, 81–82
Self-acceptance, 18–19. *See also* Subjective well-being
Self-compassion, 21, 49
Self-enhancement, 57–58
Self-kindness, 21
Self-knowledge, 106
Seligman, M. E. P., 18, 20, 65, 79
Seligowski, A. V., 22
Sense of self, 25, 81–82
Sexual assault/violence, 3
Shakespeare-Finch, J., 4, 9
Shannon, P. J., 11–12
Shared space. *See* Coworking
Shell shock, 2
Signature strengths, 104–105
Slade, M., 36
Slattery, J. M., 59–60
Smith, R. S., 56–57
Snyder, C. R., 21, 56, 65
Speechless terror, 7–8
Spiritual growth, 95
Spirituality. *See also* Religiousness
after trauma, 92–94
defined/defining, 89–91
overview, 89–90
promoting, 94–97
questions, 90
Spiritual transformation, 95
Spreitzer, G. M., 24
Spurgeon, D. W., 90
Srivastava, M., 36
Steen, T. A., 18
Steger, M. F., 77, 79
Strauss, Darin, 101
Strengths
culturally embedded, 22
signature, 104–105
temperance, 20
transcendence, 20
universal, 22
Subjective well-being, 18
aspects, 18
autonomy, 19
courage, 20
environmental mastery, 19
eudaimonic models, 18
humanity, 20
interpersonal relationships, 25
justice, 20
personal growth, 19
purpose in life, 19
self-acceptance, 18–19
temperance, 20
thriving, 105–106
transcendence, 20
wisdom, 20
Substance Abuse and Mental Health Services Administration, 55
Sullivan, B. A., 77

Suresh, D. P., 79
Symptoms of traumatized persons, 6

T
Tallman, B. A., 25, 65, 82
Tedeschi, R. G., 7–8
Temperance, 20. *See also* Subjective well-being
Ter Kuile, H., 92
Terrill, A. L., 24
Toussaint, L. L., 69
Townsdin, J., 69–70
Trajectories of life after trauma, 102–104
  delayed distress, 24
  growth, 103–104
  impairment, 24, 102
  recovery, 24, 103
  resilience, 24, 103
Transcendence, 20. *See also* Subjective well-being
Transgenerational transmission, 10
Trauma
  affecting people, 6–8
    arousal and affect regulation, 7–8
    distortion of reality, 8
    identity, 8
    immobilization/freezing, 7
  bereavement, 4
  betrayal, 9–10
  concept, 1–6
  immigration and migration, 11–12
  intimate partner violence, 4
  mass violence as, 2–3
  military trauma, 10–11
  motor vehicle accidents, 5
  natural and environmental disasters, 4
  overview, 1
  peer-to-peer violence, 3
  sexual assault, 3
  transgenerational transmission, 10
  vicarious, 9
Trauma-informed, 1
Trauma memories, 6–7
Trauma Recovery Project, 103
Traumatic stressors, 2
Trickett, P. K., 9
Trompetter, H. R., 21–22
Turgoose, D., 9
Twitter, 1

U
United States Department of Justice, 2–3
Universal view of strengths, 22
University of Texas, 2–3
Uy, K. K., 26

V
Van der Kolk, B., 7–8, 61
Vander Laan, K. L., 69
Van Ryzin, M. J., 93
Vicarious trauma, 9
Victim, 8
Vinson, G. A., 11–12
Violence. *See also* Trauma
  intimate partner, 4
  mass, 2–3
  peer-to-peer, 3
  sexual, 3

W
War trauma, 11–12
Weber, E. N., 33
Weiss, D. S., 102
Well-being. *See* Subjective well-being
Werner, E. E., 56–57
Wessely, S., 2
Weymar, M., 6
Wieling, E., 11–12
Wierzbicka, A., 22
Williams, J., 36
Wisdom, 20. *See also* Subjective well-being
Witvliet, C. V. O., 69–70
Wolf, Brandon, 101
Woodyatt, L., 69–70
Workplace bullying, 3
World War I, 2
World War II, 11, 77
Worthington, E. L., 66–67, 69
Wortman, C. B., 82
Wu, K. K., 5

Y
Yehuda, R., 10

FSC
www.fsc.org
MIX
Papier | Fördert
gute Waldnutzung
FSC® C083411

Kolibri 360 GmbH
Ferdinand-Jühlke-Straße 7
99095 Erfurt, Deutschland
produktsicherheit@kolibri360.de